Women In Prison:
Women Finding Freedom

Welcome to a wonderful opportunity to learn tools to help you create the kind of life which will afford you peace of mind. With the material in this book you have the opportunity to discover internal freedom which is the only freedom worth striving to experience. If you are incarcerated and reading this book it is because someone, somewhere donated the money to provide this information to you. Someone cares about your internal freedom. It may have been a friend or someone you don't even know who bought this book you now read. The point is....you are not alone in your journey. Someone cares about you and wants you to be internally free.

GOGI
PRAYER

Dear GOD,
Grant us the joy of giving and receiving so that our inner freedom may be of maximum service to those we love and infinite others.

Amen

Women In Prison: Women Finding Freedom

ISBN-10: 0-9786721-5-1   ISBN-13: 978-0-9786721-5-7

Disclaimer

© Cover, Logo, Images, Contributions courtesy of Getting Out by Going In
Cover Art: Jennifer Berger, GOGI Campus 2008
Cover Design: Catherine Brankov, Create Advertising
Layout: Roselle Kipp
Contributors: This publication was written with the help of the Women at GOGI Campus 2008, Lynwood, California, USA. *Thanks to everyone for your generous contribution, including, but not limited to illustrations, poems & quotations.*

For questions, e-mail <info@gettingoutbygoingin.org> or write to:
GETTING OUT BY GOING IN, PO Box 88969, Los Angeles, CA, 90009, USA

Published in the United States of America by Lightning Source, Inc.

Print is last number listed: 9 8 7 6 5 4 3 2 1

Women In Prison:
Women Finding Freedom

By COACH MARA LEIGH TAYLOR

Getting Out
By Going In ™

People Can Change!

You, too, can be Free!

LET GO, FORGIVE + CLAIM RESPONSIBILITY

Personal Tools For Internal Freedom. . .

BOSS OF YOUR BRAIN - allows you to
take control of all your thoughts and actions.

BELLY BREATHING - allows you to
take control of your entire body.

FIVE SECOND LIGHTSWITCH - allows you to
stop and think before you act.

WHAT IF? - allows you to think from a
powerful and positive perspective.

POSITIVE TWA
(Thoughts, Words, Actions)
TWA are three keys that allows
you to control your
thoughts, word, and actions.

REALITY CHECK - allows you to accept
The process of change more fully.

Foreword by Dr. Kimora

    ✍ During the early part of September, 2007, Coach Taylor and I met for the first time in New York City. We were guests on a local radio show. The subject of discussion was incarceration in the US. The host was asking a panel of experts about prison education work and if education was a way of reducing the nation's rising rates of incarceration. During the panel discussion, each of the guests responded to various questions asked by the host and the listening audience. I immediately felt a kinship with Coach Taylor. We agreed on so many aspects of correctional education. During our hour long radio show, we were attempting to convince the radio audience that teaching offenders basic cognitive skills would reduce crime and aid them in their return as productive members of society.

    The following May, 2008, I was invited by Coach Taylor to visit GOGI Campus, a unique reentry program. She asked me to speak with her "GOGI Girls", female jail inmates volunteering to participate in a unique reentry program offered by the Los Angeles County Sheriff Department. GOGI Campus is a place where inmates learn tools for positive decision making. At GOGI Campus, the participating inmates are called "students" and their first names are used in communication with their "Coaches". Through a team of community volunteers and psychology students, the GOGI Girls are taught the very tools you will read in this book. Not surprisingly, the first six months of the program there was zero recidivism among inmates completing the program.

    During my visit, it was wonderful to see how Coach Taylor was able to connect with the incarcerated women and provide them with concrete solutions to their poor decision making. I have not encountered too many people who know how to relate to those who are incarcerated.

I have worked as a correctional educator in jails, prisons, halfway houses and drug treatment centers in Minnesota, California and New York for over twenty-three years. During that time I have encountered many people who abuse and oppress those who they "care" for in the criminal justice system. It was refreshing to see a person lead a team of volunteers and the incarcerated women on a very positive journey of self-discovery and educational enrichment.

As of June 2007, the United States Department of Justice reports 2,299,116 prisoners held in federal or state prisons or in local jails. This is an increase of 1.8% from the yearend 2006. The number of women under the jurisdiction of state or federal prison authorities increased 2.5% from yearend 2006, reaching 115,308. The number of men rose 1.5%, totaling 1,479,726. Ours is a Nation of massive incarceration. Something must change.

Over the years, I experienced firsthand knowledge that very few educational programs exist for women in prison. Incarcerated women are lucky if they have access to a basket weaving course or an AA meeting. That is about the extent of the correctional education that is offered to them. This is a pitiful situation in a land that incarcerates more people than any other nation on the planet. You would think the United States would have the insight and forethought to educate incarcerated women so when they are released, they can become productive members of society.

I fully endorse WOMEN IN PRISON: Women Finding Freedom by Coach Mara Leigh Taylor as a powerful tool for all incarcerated women. In the book, Coach Taylor is engaging all of us in a conversation that is long overdue in this nation. You and I, incarcerated or not, can enrich our lives by learning to embrace the simple GOGI tools which are allowing incarcerated women to take control of their lives in a positive way. You and I know that when we all embrace a positive

outlook (with tools to actualize realistic, humanitarian outcomes) we are getting closer to reversing recidivism and bringing this planet together in peaceful coexistence. ❧

Peace,
Professor Kimora
John Jay College of Criminal Justice, NYC
kimora@jjay.cuny.eduSeptember, 2008

When everything that can possibly go wrong...
When you don't think you can keep going on...
When your depression & guilt start to take you down...
When you want to give up...Don't!!! Breathe!!!
Belly Breathe, take a deep breath.
Things are going to get better.

Words from Coach Taylor...

❧   I have never been incarcerated in the way we commonly define incarceration. My incarceration was socially invisible, subtle, and unseen but it was no less real, no less debilitating and no less restricting. I came to my calling of working with prisoners by accident. When my psychology class took a tour of a Federal Prison, we students were led throughout the facility and into the classrooms not unlike school kids visiting a zoo. The men didn't like being put on display which you could tell by their expressions.

What I found oddly comforting was the way that their physical world resembled my internal world in a visceral sense. Prison looked like how I felt inside. Some part of me knew if I were able to help prisoners find internal freedom that somewhere along the way I would find my own. My internal freedom came through my service to others.

Along this journey, I continue to learn a bit about freedom. Do you know what is interesting? I have never met a convicted man, woman or child who said they meditated and prayed on the day they committed a crime or were arrested. I have not met any convicts who committed crimes on their way back from church, a volunteer job, an AA meeting, or from helping someone in need.

I have not met many individuals who remembered they were the BOSS OF THEIR BRAIN and then went out and violated a law. I have not met many women who really practiced BELLY BREATHING and went out and got drunk. I have not met many young mothers who understood and practiced FIVE SECOND LIGHT SWITCH and then were arrested for child endangerment. I have not met many people who robbed a liquor store on their way home from night school to get a GED.

The point is...there are practical things you can do every day to free yourself. You can do many things to stay out *of harm's way. Sober & Sane. Many, many simple things you can do today. You can begin your day with a prayer and then remember that prayer all day long. Live that prayer. Meditate for a moment or two when the urge gets strong to use or react in that old way. Be of service to a non-profit organization or church. Go to school. Attend meetings, ANY meetings, where sober people gather. Go to church, ANY church.*

Successful reentry into your community is only one decision away. It is a decision to walk beyond the wreckage of your past. Do what sober women do. Think like sober women think. Speak like sober women speak. Serve like sober women serve. And always remember, jails and prisons are filled with people who chose to be in an environment which was not conducive to sobriety, honesty, integrity, and spirituality.

I have great faith in your big, huge, open hearts. And I know the intensity of emotion you feel is both a blessing and a curse. It can disable you and it can empower you as well. The information in this book is designed to protect that heart by having you make positive decisions. Make blessings out of the curses of your life. Use this time in confinement as a time for reconstruction of self.

What would your life be like if you truly never used a drug again? What would your life be like if you never drank alcohol again? What would your life be like if you never took anyone's identity, if you never risked a child's life, if you didn't take the fall for a man? What would your life be like if you found that place of internal freedom which is only found through being a sober woman of integrity? What if you got it "right" this time? You can do it. Let the tools in this book help you be the brave warrior for good that you were meant to become. ❧

What is a GOGI Girl?

Throughout this book you will see the art and read the words of GOGI Girls. A GOGI Girl is a woman who refuses to let the wreckage of her past define her future. She is any woman who has suffered the emotional, physical and spiritual pain of incarceration but refuses to let that be an excuse for future failures. A GOGI Girl is any woman who is willing to GET OUT of old behavior by GOING IN to personal responsibility and personal accountability.

In 2008, the first GOGI Campus was opened under the permission and support of the Los Angeles County Sheriff's Department. A total of 24 female inmates were the first "students" in the class of '08 and were called "GOGI Girls." What has occurred since that humble beginning in the East Tower of CRDF 2200 Pod 4 has been nothing short of a miracle.

Let me share with you the story of Jilly. Jilly had a long running drug addiction. When she entered GOGI Campus and learned the very tools you will learn in this book, she decided she was "over" the self destruction of her life. She was finally ready to make a stand for getting herself sober. She received a court order for a drug treatment program, but when she was released from the county jail, there was no mandate for her to go to the treatment facility. She could have done what she always did and she would get what she always got. She could have called her boyfriend who had just gotten out of jail. He would have picked her up and they would soon be back to getting high and running low on money. Instead, she made a stand for her sobriety and she refused to leave the jail unless she was delivered directly to a treatment center. "I have been down this road before. I can't do it. I must get to a treatment center," she told the releasing officer. Perplexed by this ex-inmate's insistence on remaining exactly where she was until she could be picked up by a treatment center; Jilly was finally making a stand for herself. She was brave enough to do things differently and insist on a "sober only" mandate in her life.

The Los Angeles County Sheriff's Department accommodated her strong stand for her well being. Officer Rivera stayed well after his shift to make certain Jilly got to a treatment center safely. That is a true GOGI Girl, someone who has learned the tools for making positive decisions and someone who is making a stand for their sobriety, sanity, and integrity.

Here is the story of Laura W., the class president of GOGI Campus ~ Lynwood. Laura had the chance to leave GOGI Campus to begin her prison term. The sooner she left GOGI Campus the sooner she would get home and get on with her life. Laura asked her judge to grant a six month continuance of her sentencing, postponing her prison term for this amount of time. In asking for this continuance, she added six additional months to her stay behind bars.

Laura is a true GOGI Girl. She wanted to do whatever it took to guarantee that she had all the tools necessary to walk beyond the wreckage of addiction, even if it meant six additional months behind bars.

One last GOGI Girl story; Jennifer B. Jennifer B was court ordered to a treatment center but they had no bed for her. She was last on their list because she had walked away from that very same facility a few years ago, and the manager was not too thrilled to have her back. Jennifer, however, had learned the GOGI tools.

She was the Boss of her Brain now and ready for a real life. Instead of waiting a month or more for a bed space to open, Jennifer B showed up each and every morning asking if she could sit in on the groups or help in any way possible. Soon they realized Jennifer was finally ready and they immediately opened a bed for her. Jennifer did not let "no" stop her from making a stand for her sobriety and sanity.

GOGI Girls appear to do some pretty crazy things: refuse to leave jail, extend their time behind bars and even show up at treatment centers volunteering to help until a bed opens up.

A true GOGI Girl will make every effort to secure a life of integrity and sobriety. Can you be a GOGI Girl? Yes. All you need to do is learn the tools in this book and then do whatever it takes ~ and I do mean WHATEVER IT TAKES ~ to secure a sober, sane, life of integrity.

We welcome you to the journey of the GOGI Girl. The tools are here and the freedom is waiting inside you. You can do it. You can drastically, radically, and permanently change your life for the better. Read this book, share the tools with others, and commit to a sober-only existence.

They may be able to lock you behind bars for your bad decisions but they cannot take away your ability to create a profound internal freedom for yourself, no matter where you wake up each morning.

Coach Taylor
Founder / President
GETTING OUT BY GOING IN

Acknowledgements

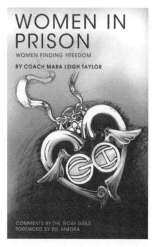

GOGI has been blessed. From the beginning workshop held at Terminal Island Federal prison in 2002 up until today, the inmates who participate in all GOGI activities and workshops have been actively involved and interested in change.

It is because of these inmates that GOGI is successful. GETTING OUT BY GOING IN is an organization dedicated to the education and empowerment of incarcerated men, women and children. In a very real way, we help inmates help themselves.

This book, *Women in Prison: Women Finding Freedom*, would not have been possible were it not for the 150 incarcerated women who participated in the year long GOGI Campus pilot program, a unique community collaboration reentry project at the county jail in Los Angeles County.

The GOGI Campus pilot program would not have been possible without the permission and vision of members of the Los Angeles County Sheriff's Department.

GOGI Campus is my vision for all settings of incarceration; an environment which promotes and supports the good in all humans. GOGI Campus was designed to radically reduce recidivism. It worked.

After six months, not one of our graduates was rearrested. Zero percent recidivism. At this printing in December 2008, GOGI Campus has a 2.5 recidivism rate among our graduates. That means 97.5 percent of our graduates remain in society and have broken the cycle of lifelong recidivism.

GOGI Campus owes a great deal to Los Angeles County Sheriff's Department Sergeant Grady Machnick. He approached me while I signed GOGI books at the Los Angeles Times Book Fair. In his charge to seek out, identify and support successful re-entry programs, we collaborated in putting together a program to empower individuals with the tools and support for positive decision making. I was invited to present the concept to the Los Angeles County Sheriff's Department. I was blessed to be assigned Deputy Roel Garcia as my point person. Roel has become a valued friend and a man I respect and trust.

Grady and Roel have been GOGI Champions, honorary GOGI Coaches; champions of change. Without these two visionaries, I would not have been able to withstand the inherent challenges we faced. I am forever grateful to Deputy Roel Garcia and Sgt Grady Machnick, educator Barbara Walker and everyone at the Los Angeles County Sheriff's Department who invested personal time and energy into the success of the GOGI Campus pilot program.

To the GOGI Girls, the first "graduating" class of GOGI Campus 2008, You Did It! YOU proved that providing the correct environment and support, people can, want and will change. "You are GOGI Girls, in a GOGI World." Laura W., thank you. You were the finest Class President any campus could have.

To more than 700 male inmates at facilities across America who have or are participating or leading their own GOGI classes and correspondence courses, God bless you and thank you.

To all the GOGI Coaches, thank you. Coach DJ, Eddie W., A. Gordon, Eddie P., Kevin W. and the GOGI men of CMC and Jeff and the vets of San Quentin, thank you for being powerful forces for positive change.

To the increasing numbers of correspondence students in state and federal facilities, thank you. Bless you all. GOGI sees and supports your goodness.

Recidivism and drug abuse is an increasing concern for the citizens of the US and at the end of 2008 we had more than two million men, women and children behind bars. Locking people up is not the answer.

With the success of GOGI Campus, at long last, administrations are looking at the possibility that just locking away the problem may actually create additional problems. Solutions are available. They are simple, cost effective, and morally correct. It is our vision to have a GOGI Campus in every setting of incarceration across the nation.

No matter where you are, the human experience can be positive, good, kind and loving. It is never too late to choose good over evil, kindness over brutality. Thanks to all of you who understand how simple it is to turn the course of life. Thank you.

Coach Taylor with friend and fellow GOGI Coach, Doctor Kimora.

GOGI Girl Dee Dee Z. and Family.

Coach Judy, Coach Dorene and Coach Tanya pause for a picture outside GOGI Campus in Lynwood, California.

All GOGI Coaches participate in training which helps them qualify as psychologists, drug treatment counselors, and social workers.

Women In Prison: Women Finding Freedom
TABLE OF CONTENTS

There are many ways to make changes in your life. Listed below are some tips from GOGI Girls. Set your own pace. If you are willing to practice these concepts and tools every day, a little each day, you can make certain that the changes you WANT to make -- are the changes that you ACTUALLY MAKE HAPPEN!

1) Read this book (and all books, for that matter) with a pencil nearby. Write thoughts that you have in the margins of the book if it is yours, or on paper. Writing helps the brain remember things.

2) When you finish each chapter set the book down. Write a letter and share what you have learned in that chapter. If you don't write letters then write down notes for yourself about the chapter. Thinking, pondering and writing gets the information into your brain cells forever.

3) Re-read the chapter again to see what you might have missed on the first reading. This provides even deeper learning.

4) Once you have read the entire book, open it up again and start from the beginning and re-read every word. Layers of skills and talents are built with repetition.

5) Observe others who display natural skills with the tools described. Watch what they do, what they say.

6) Share the ideas on telephone calls or on visits with family, children, and friends. Teaching is the final step in learning.

7) Share or give the book to someone. Help teach them how you applied the tools in your life. Giving is the acknowledgement of completion.

CHAPTER 1

RELEASE PREPARATION

Freedom Awaits You...

Welcome to the journey of getting out of your prison before your release from physical confinement. What we know is experiencing internal freedom is possible for any imprisoned individual, irrespective of the walls defining the physical confinement.

Whether your prison is a State penitentiary, a Bureau of Prisons (BOP) facility, a jail, a dead-end job, an economic hardship, a bad marriage, a disabled body, or an addiction - it is possible for you to create the unique experience of internal freedom. You can "get out" of the habits and decision-making ruts that may have led to your time behind bars.

What is available to you during "lock-up" is an unlimited potential for internal freedom. You are able to internalize changes without the chaos of life or the limits that were created by habits and behaviors which hamper your progress.

No one wants to be behind bars. But confinement provides a rare opportunity to focus and dramatically change your life by doing things differently.

Even if you might be told how to dress, how and where to stand, or even how and why to walk, the powerful truth is that **no one, absolutely no one,** can tell you what or how to think. No one can limit your internal freedom.

The way you think *is* your personal journey toward internal freedom. It *is* your set of keys out of prison. While incarcerated you have the opportunity to master, if you will, the fine art of internal freedom.

Words from GOGI Girl Angel H.
What does GOGI mean to me?
Letting go of the old and embracing a new you

What if you imagined your incarceration as a college or a scientific laboratory for you to experiment with your own internal change? This laboratory would make increasing amounts of freedom available to you. You can choose to take steps inward to your own soul's strength, goodness and intelligence.

You have the opportunity to experiment, test, learn, and grow while behind bars and ultimately free yourself. **Internal freedom is available to everyone**, even if very few actually make it their priority.

The internal journey towards internal freedom requires focus and dedication. It takes time and effort, and is oftentimes absent immediate gratification. It can be a lonely trail, testing your internal fortitude beyond all reasonable bounds. Many free people live and die in prison, limited by fear, anger, resentment, and blame others for their own plight. You have a unique opportunity to walk beyond these walls and find internal freedom.

The material that GETTING OUT BY GOING IN offers is also consistent with religious and spiritual practices that are universally empowering for practitioners.

> ♥A torrent of forces work against successful re-entry and yet, sometimes all a person needs is a roadmap with information, support and opportunity. The tools contained in this GOGI Book are intended to provide that roadmap for you. You <u>can</u> change and GOGI is here to remind you!♥
>
> Coach Taylor

Most importantly is the simple fact that the material in this book provides practical tools. They may enable you to put basic spiritual concepts and self-improvement concepts into **action for yourself**.

These concepts and tools represent portions of the GOGI curriculum designed for incarcerated individuals. They combine an overview of the body's physiological operation (BODY), the mind's complex simplicity (MIND) and the human spirit's resiliency (SPIRIT).

The material provides assistance for you to gain internal freedom during your everyday experiences behind bars. It is also likely that this information can increase your success after your release. In other words, you can choose to utilize these tools to create a powerfully successful, happy life for yourself, regardless of where you lay your head at night.

Change is an individual process. Change cannot be forced, nor can it be mandated as a release requirement. Internal change is possible during incarceration but is not a guarantee of the process.

Words from Coach Taylor...

     🌀 *I have come to realize that making good choices is just a habit. If you have a habit of making bad decisions, it is likely you will have run into the law again and again and again. If you begin to create new habits which are positive, it is inevitable that you will change your life forever.*

     If your daily life is just a set of habits, can you think of some habits that you could change or replace? What about when you get angry when a person says something that seems unfair? What about when you get discouraged when things seem too difficult? What about when you do not want to feel alone so you run to the bottle? What about when you get frustrated and return back to familiar ways of doing things?

     What you think is likely a habit that you formed. What if you made a new habit? What if every time your eyes opened you had the habit of saying a prayer, smiling, meditating, doing sit-ups? What if you made a new habit to relax instead of getting uptight?

     These are all habits. It is just as easy to form a bad habit as it is a good habit. People who have good habits create more good habits easily. People with bad habits create more bad habits easily.

     It is your job to start developing good habits. Once you have enough good habits they will start increasing on their own. Habits, good or bad, are yours to develop. It is your life. Start to count your good habits and keep adding to them until they become self-generating. You can do it. 🌀

Happy.

THE CONTRIBUTION OF CLINICAL PSYCHOLOGY

Several clinical psychology modalities were used in the formulation of techniques used in this material. While psychologically based, the techniques in the GOGI curriculum are simple, understandable and organic to the individual experience.

The techniques are uniquely combined but not in a "secret combination." Some prefer scientific evidence, a religious foundation, or to see the tools in action. Some only get motivated to change by reading comments from a GOGI Girl. Individuals pick and choose what fits their particular style of learning.

The RapidChange Therapy (RCT) methodology, used in developing the GOGI techniques, is based on the belief that understandable information (referred to as DATA) must be provided within a context.

This new context (referred to as SPACE) is where the individual can draw alternative conclusions and develop new cognitions, or ways of thinking.

The combination of SPACE + DATA + a perceptual SHIFT leads to new behaviors (CHANGE.) Therefore, the formula for lasting change is:

$$SPACE + DATA + SHIFT = CHANGE$$

RapidChange Therapy techniques and theories are designed to help you by:

- Creating optimal SPACE for this information to be tested and practiced.
- This SPACE affords the individual perceptual SHIFTS of thinking and awareness.
- Providing DATA in the form of understandable information.
- And, supporting the inevitable CHANGE which occurs as a result of DATA and SPACE and perceptual SHIFT availability.

In other words, GETTING OUT BY GOING IN has found that the concepts of RapidChange Therapy helps the GOGI coaches as they help others to help themselves.

The RapidChange Therapy Formula for Change:

SPACE + DATA + SHIFT = CHANGE

SPACE is mental room to consider the information.
DATA is information. This gives you the opportunity for perceptual SHIFT.
CHANGE is the new habits which form.

GOGI uses RapidChange Therapy to empower at-risk and incarcerated individuals to make powerful decisions.

Art by Davida M.

This book is based on techniques of RapidChange Therapy (RCT), which is a unique psychological modality for rapid and lasting change. It combines traditional clinical psychology, universal human ethics and time-proven strategies for success. RCT allows for rapid change in thinking and behavior; and is the synthesis of tools for the Body, Mind and Spirit.

If asked to define RapidChange Therapy, it is helpful to call upon well-known psychological theories that are similar: Cognitive Behavioral Therapy (CBT) is similar to RapidChange Therapy. Both are based on the fact that cognitions (understanding) and behaviors are teamed to promote change. Solutions Focused Therapy is similar to RapidChange Therapy because both theories focus on the goal, or intended outcome. Brief Therapy is similar to RapidChange Therapy because it does not take a long time to get change to happen. Brief therapy does not require deep discussions of the "etiology" (a psychological term for origin) of a problem.

RapidChange Therapy is a blend of successful psychological theories and is at the core of the GOGI curriculum and intent. It presents techniques which are global in their effectiveness and is a WAY of making change happen. RapidChange Therapy supports the GOGI goals of empowering individuals to make positive decisions in their lives. It is not exclusive to the setting of incarceration. RapidChange Therapy can be used with any individual and just about any of life's challenges.

So the journey begins...

Hopefully, you accept and welcome the intent of this book. It can empower you to realize that life can be amazing, enjoyable, beneficial, productive and peaceful, regardless of where you wake up each morning.

The information lays the foundation for you to begin this portion of the journey toward internal freedom — and get out of prison before your release.

GETTING OUT BY GOING IN (GOGI) is the non-profit organization that sponsors this book. GOGI was named for the process of GETTING OUT of prison by GOING IN to the freedom only found inside of you. The material is based on volunteer work with hundreds of inmates who offered input and suggested modifications. Their insight helped form the simplicity of the tools presented.

We can all find internal freedom regardless of what kind of prison we are in. It could be a prison of addiction, negative attitude, unproductive habits, or the inability to move beyond pain and anguish. It could be the prison of a harmful relationship, the absence of love, or the limits of a broken and disabled body.

Whatever prison confines you, there is a freedom residing within. How speedily you embrace your own internal freedom is for you to determine. This material is offered to anyone who is interested in their potential for internal freedom.

CHAPTER 2

YOU CAN CHANGE

GETTING OUT BY GOING IN or GOGI (Pronounced Go-Gee like Yogi Bear) focuses on three areas of self-awareness and psychological development in a series of workshops, lectures, books, workbooks, group and individual discussions.

It takes an inward awareness and growth of the Body, Mind and Spirit to create the opportunity for internal freedom. The good news for you is that internal freedom is available to all individuals. It is free of charge. It is your birthright, and it is far more satisfying than any other human state of being. All it takes is unwavering dedication, singular focus and a solid commitment to change your life.

Changing your life must be a matter of life and death. It must be so important that no amount of suffering, struggle or obstacle can knock you off your path. The tools presented in this book are designed to offer the opportunity for growth through expansion of skills and understanding. The tools are designed with truth at the core; it takes growth in the three areas of Body, Mind and Spirit for lasting internal freedom to be realized.

1) BODY – Educating participants with a basic working comprehension of the physiological process of thought and actions is the goal of this book. When an individual learns why thoughts take place and how they affect the body and resulting reactions, they are empowered to make stronger decisions. In a very real sense, knowledge is power.

2) MIND – The goal of this book is also to provide cognitive tools, or those tools that help participants build a new understanding. This will help modify perception of available options and almost always results in behavioral change. Understanding how the mind functions and how to empower your mind for personal freedom is an essential step in getting out of prison before your release.

3) SPIRIT – Finally, the goal of this book includes making the leap from existing with a fear-based, myopic, single focused or limited perspective, to a more global interpretation of options and strategies for success. This broadened view results in the ability to build rapport with others, increase social functioning and positively enhances the capability for lasting relationships necessary to support success.

Words from Coach Taylor...

❧ Here is what I have noticed. Most incarcerated women feel inspired to change pretty quickly. They get tired of making mistakes and paying the consequences. The challenge for most women is not resistance to change. Most women want to change. The challenge is that they do not have the patience for the natural change process. Change takes time to become a habit. Most of the women I have met get frustrated with the process. They want to change but they want fast-food change. They want to see it now. But that is not how it happens.

Muscles develop over time. Repeat the process over and over again, even when there is no foreseeable benefit.

cont.

You have to practice the new habit even when you feel it is not working.

You know what? The cycle of bad decisions is just a cycle of bad habits in decision making. And the cycle of bad decisions is likely a result of a low self-esteem. When a woman has a low self-esteem it is difficult to do the internal work required to make new habits. Women with low self-esteem have a challenge in knowing they are worth the effort. They give up. They do not feel they can do it. They feel powerless to change their life.

So, what happens is women get all excited about change but then nothing happens. They often don't have the stamina, the long-term inner strength, to make change happen for a long period of time.

If this is true for you then there is a simple answer. Develop your muscles - your internal muscles. You must develop patience with the process. Stay the course. Do not get discouraged. Do not get depressed that you see no results in the process. It takes time.

How can you do this? Develop patience. Did you pray today? That helps. Did you meditate? Sit quietly? Did you read a book designed to help you improve? Did you choose words that helped others feel powerful? Did you choose words that helped you feel worthy and strong?

Right now you can begin to develop the muscles you need to build your self-esteem and start making good decisions. Once you make one good decision you can make another and another and another. Then, you will be able to teach others how to get out of their cycle of making bad decisions. ❧

BUT CAN CHANGE TRULY LAST?

Lasting change requires commitment, support and consistent reinforcement until new neurological habits of cognition and behavior are solidified within the human physiology.

Yes, change can truly last. Change can last a lifetime. Once the desired changes take place, additional opportunities to support the new behavior must be available. The RapidChange Therapy Equation for Change (SPACE + DATA + SHIFT = CHANGE) includes the need for adequate support of the change in order to maintain the desired results.

WHO CAN CHANGE?

Change is possible for. . .Small children, teenagers, adults, aging adults, blacks, whites, smokers, non-smokers, Christians, Muslims, Jews, Agnostics, Atheists, Romanians, Hungarians, Gypsies, overweights, underweights, addicts, AA members, bowlers, stamp collectors, readers, non-readers, Asians, Hispanics, Indians, American Indians, Canadians, Europeans, Australians, gays, lesbians, non-English speaking, English speaking, single moms, single dads, couples, families, inmates, former inmates, convicts, preachers, politicians, guards, teachers, anger issue individuals, the employed and the unemployed, the happy and the sad, and all those who may not fall into the categories mentioned above.

Be A Star
Shine Bright
MEGAN C.

WHAT IF IT SEEMS TOO DIFFICULT FOR ME? ▨

If the community or family environment is not supportive of your change, or unable to help you, the burden of your change will be completely on you. You can do it, however. You **can** make it. You can review the material regularly as a consistent reinforcement of the SPACE + DATA + SHIFT = CHANGE equation.

In the setting of incarceration, graduates of the GETTING OUT BY GOING IN course are often encouraged to become "Peer Coaches" and mentor or teach others within their communities. The process of the "student" becoming the "teacher" is widely recognized as a successful support strategy and further solidifies lasting change.

If you are *serious* about making lasting changes in your life you can teach what you have learned to your Bunkie, your child, your partner, your husband, or your neighbor. A powerful way to support your change is to offer the teaching to your family. Tell them about the tools when you send them letters or speak with them at visits or on the telephone.

You may find they begin to appreciate your subtle commitment to creating a powerfully positive life for yourself. You may inspire them to become more successful in their own lives.

CAN I SUCCESSFULLY CHANGE?   ？？？

Yes. Anyone anywhere can successfully change. There are, however, predictors of success, or elements or situations that show up as indicators of probable success.

The following "Predictors of Success," in the GOGI program are based on participant self reports and clinical observation of more than 500 incarcerated individuals.

Words from Coach Taylor…

൦ *Change lasts as long as you are making the decisions which support that change. You can remain thin as long as you continue to make the choices of a thin person. You can remain sober as long as you make the decisions sober women make. You can remain calm as long as you make the decisions similar to the ones those calm women make.*

Change lasts as long as you support the change with your choices. And, if you choose not to drink that drink then you are supporting sobriety. If you choose not to yell you are supporting your relaxation. If you choose not to overeat you are choosing to support your thin body. The positive change you want can be supported in your decisions today. Positive change lasts.

And, bad habits last, too. They last just as long as you make decisions which support bad habits. If you are thinking about that next hit you are supporting that bad habit. If you are thinking about yelling at someone you are supporting your anger. If you are thinking about easy money, lying about something, cheating, stealing, using, and drinking then you are supporting those habits.

What you choose to think about this very minute tells your body what habit you want. And what you say throughout the day tells your body what habit you want. What you choose to feel tells your body what habit you want. If you want to change your habits you will need to change the thoughts, the words and the actions you choose.

The good news is that habits are choices. You can choose to be a sober woman by building sober habits. ൦

Women who found internal freedom and have been successful in the process of change are most likely to be:

1) Women Who Enjoy a Broad Range of Experiences.

Successful women apply the GOGI tools and RapidChange Therapy techniques across a broad range of experiences for full integration.

You will be more successful if you look at your entire life from the perspective of the tools. It will help if you apply the tools throughout your day in all circumstances to obtain maximum benefits. If you only apply the tools in certain environments, for example with your Bunkie and not the C.O., you are limiting your growth.

2) Women Who Enjoy a Broad Range of Relationships.

Successful women apply the GOGI techniques when interacting with family members, prison staff or others during work and even on phone conversations.

Successful women practice new ways of listening, speaking and reacting with a wide group of people. This permits competencies in areas previously considered weak or needing work.

3) Women Who Share Information.

Sharing the techniques and information affirms new learning. Women who teach or explain the process to others are far more likely to integrate the GOGI tools into their daily lives.

Art by Taylor W.

Words from Coach Taylor...

෨ *Your friends. What do they talk about? Do they talk about reading a good book? Going to church? Finishing school? Do your friends talk about getting a good job and doing what it takes to advance in the company? Do they talk about how they are building new habits to be a better person? Are they all talk and no action? Do your friends talk about wanting to help others and telling you of how they helped someone that day? Do your friends ask how your reading, study or good habits are helping you?*

Your ability to be a friend. Do you support the good decisions of your friends or do you gossip about how wrong a person was? Do you complain and listen to complaints or do you compliment? Do you help your friends make better decisions or do you listen to the long list of reasons why they were wronged?

Who are you? Are you a woman who stands as an example of self improvement or are you just like everybody else.... Blaming the system. Blaming the man. Blaming the money. Blaming the addiction. "I can't."

Who do you want to be? Do you even want to be powerful? Sober? Or, do you want to live a life of blaming everyone but yourself? Ask yourself. Are you willing to be bigger than the situation? Or do you need to hold tightly to making everyone see how wrong they are?

Are you ready to live? Because if you are, it takes effort. It is not easy. But, it can be done easily when you make sober choices. ෨

Megan C.

WHAT ABOUT FAMILY INVOLVEMENT?

In many cases, family involvement proves to be the most positive determining factor in the long-term success of re-unification, especially among adolescents, teens, and young adults. Having a supportive family helps all individuals. Families may not know how to adequately support fundamental changes when loved ones return home. Old and destructive patterns might naturally resurface, and it becomes nearly impossible to sustain positive change. You must be very committed to new habits and not let the behaviors of others pull you off track. If your family, your job, your neighborhood, and/or your environment cannot support you, then you must support yourself fully, totally, completely.

Family members might have a difficult time thinking of you in any other way than how you used to be. For as long as you have been down, they may still remember that "old" version. However, it is possible for them to see the "new" version, so do not be discouraged.

It is challenging for anyone to see that someone has changed. For some reason we humans tend to feel comfortable with what we are familiar with, even if it is not the best trait or situation. If your family does not recognize or support the desired change, they may box you into a situation, which can steer you to old behavior.

Upon completion of this book, you are encouraged to integrate the GOGI tools in the home environment - with willing family members. You may decide to keep the GETTING OUT BY GOING IN book and other self-help books in your library of support. Think about getting a copy of this book to your family as it can be a start for them to see the "new" you before you go home.

Sending letters to family with ideas on how to use the GOGI tools or other self-empowerment techniques is one way to get them used to a new you. Teaching a family member some of the techniques is a start at developing their support for your new learning. Sharing positive stories of success while you are incarcerated and making lasting changes in your life is a solid start at getting the home front to support your changes.

Long before you get home, your task is to have your family understand and accept you for the changes that you have made. Teaching your family some of the tools at your disposal may prove to be strengthening positive support for change upon your release.

WHAT IF THERE IS NO FORMAL GOGI "CLASS" AND I AM READING THIS BOOK ON MY OWN?

In all learning environments, materials and course experience is enhanced by the instructor's delivery. If you are reading the book on your own, you can take the role of being your own "Coach." You can play the role that GETTING OUT BY GOING IN coaches provide when facilitating any of the GOGI workshops.

Much like a coach of a sports team, the first step is to set firm goals and stick to your desire for internal freedom. You may set the goal not to let a situation consume your thoughts, to become calmer, or to seek increased internal peace. Each of these qualities is on the path toward internal freedom.

Whatever your goal is, keep your focus clear and your intent sound. Use the tools described in the book much like a carpenter uses tools to build a home. You may wish to write yourself a note you keep by your bunk. You may wish to keep a note in your pocket as a little reminder. You may wish to create a mantra, a meditation, a prayer or an affirmation that supports the path that you've chosen to boost your empowerment.

Words from Coach Taylor...

    ☞ *Going it alone. So many women avoid the feeling of being alone. They get lonely, depressed, or angry when they feel as if they are alone. This is unfortunate because it is almost always when we are alone with our thoughts and our feelings that we are able to figure things out for ourselves. When we clutter our lives with the voices of others, we oftentimes listen to those voices. The real problem is the fact that we pick the wrong voices, the voices of those who are not successful.*

    Many women, especially women with drug or alcohol addictions, keep themselves busy trying not to be alone. In doing so, they avoid opportunities to grow. So, we get well-meaning women who are afraid to feel lonely long enough to hear their own answers. It's a shame because women are stronger than they think. They are smarter than they think. And they are far more capable than they think.

    Being alone and feeling lonely may allow you to decide, once and for all, how you want your life to unfold. ∾

Art by Davida M.

Words from Coach Taylor...

❧ *Classrooms are oftentimes the place where we learn the least. There are too many people. The noise is too loud. The questions don't pertain to what you need to know. But in the stillness of prayer, or the stillness of meditation, the questions and the answers are exclusively yours.*

Do not discount the value of sitting still for ten minutes and just allowing your body to breathe. Do not discount the power of your prayers of gratitude. Do not discount the importance of reading a book, taking a walk in the yard, or finding some quiet time alone.

Try it today. Just sit on your bed/bunk and close your eyes for a few minutes. Concentrate on your breathing. See if you can follow the air in through your nose and then out. See if you can concentrate on your breathing so all other thoughts disappear.

The finest classroom in the world is found when you are relaxed and in a meditative space. There are worlds for you to explore within the safety of your alone time. ❧

Words from GOGI Girl Laura W.

I used to have a recurring nightmare all through my childhood. I was a little girl lost in a field of flowers taller than me. In the distance, I could see a rooftop of a house where I longed to be; however, I was stuck on this path in that field following my dog. I was going nowhere because this path went in a never-ending circle. I'd get fearful and frustrated trying to get off this path and head toward my destination, the house.

I now realize this path was that of the circle of self-destruction and addiction. I am now on the path of self betterment, my healing has begun with the awareness that I don't need to try to do anything or get anywhere. The home that I always longed for but was afraid to walk through the fears to get to was right inside of me all the time. I am now home in my own skin...

Words from Coach Taylor...

❧ *The finest thing you can do is to get to a point where you can GOGI Coach yourself. You can do this. It's not difficult. Just pretend that you have a coach whispering in your ear. Before you react to something you can ask yourself, "If a GOGI Coach were right here, right now, what would they suggest that I do?"*

When we are able to Coach ourselves, we are empowered to make better decisions. The challenge comes because many women give up their right to GOGI Coach themselves. They let drugs take over. They let a man take over. They let their emotions take over. They let what someone says about them take over. They let their past failures take over. It is very easy to change when we let the voice of our inner "GOGI Coach" guide you toward positive decisions.

Try it... If someone upsets you, before you react you can ask yourself, "What would a GOGI Coach suggest that I do right now?" I bet you will find a better answer than if you let your emotions make the decision for you.

I am a GOGI Coach by profession, but that does not mean that I don't have the same struggle as you. I have just gotten into the habit of asking before I react. I ask myself, "what would I suggest a client to do right now?"

Deep inside, we all know the answers which support our soul and our physical and spiritual well being. We all know what is right. And, we can all create new habits to support what we know is right. Start asking your personal GOGI Coach for suggestions before you react. You might find your response to events and circumstances becomes quite positive and powerful. Before you know it, your positive decisions will become more and more natural to you. Easier. It does get easier. ❧

MEG C.

WHAT IS THE PURPOSE OF THIS BOOK?

From the very first GETTING OUT BY GOING IN class held at Federal Prison in California, it has been the goal of GOGI to empower individuals to make decisions, which bring internal joy, peace and happiness.

The techniques and concepts in this book have helped people with bad tempers to rapidly deal with their temper. The techniques have helped people to overcome feeling ashamed of their lives or situations and begin to teach others powerful techniques of internal freedom. These techniques and concepts have helped people who are locked away from their children become involved in their children's lives.

This book is designed to provide tools to help make your life wonderful - right now, today, and at this very moment. It is likely that your experience of integrating and diligently living the concepts of these simple tools will result in a successful, lasting re-entry into society. More important than lasting successful re-entry, is the internal freedom available to you right this very minute, this very day. Optimally, your life will be a force for good. You can become one of those increasingly frequent individuals who are helping yourself by setting a powerful example for a positive and simple life.

When you become successful at this thing called life, your internal freedom will be profound, and your environment will benefit from your gentle walk on earth. When you are successful at this thing called life, your positive influence will be felt wherever you find yourself.

Words from Coach Taylor...

    ❧ *Will it work for you? Only if you are willing to make the choices a sober woman makes. One choice at a time. Sober choices. And it works if you are willing to nurture these new decisions until they become your new habits. It works if you work, too.*❧

Words from Coach Taylor...

❧ *Who you are is determined with each and every word you choose. If I was a negative drug user in the past, that does not mean that I need to be an angry drug user today. Today I can be peaceful. Today I can pray. Today I can meditate. I can do 50 sit-ups today. I can touch my toes and stretch my body today. I can eat less junk today. I can drink more water today.*

What I do today sends a message to my entire body and my mind. It makes a declaration of who I am choosing to be, this very moment. The challenge for most women is that they drag their past into their future with them. Then they try to fix the past, make it better. Well, that is like taking an overcooked stew and trying to make it taste good by adding new ingredients. The new ingredients take on the burnt flavor.

Why not walk away from the behaviors of the past, the burned up and destructive stew, and cook up some new possibilities? Today you have 24 hours. What if 23 of them were spent testing out the GOGI tools? What if you chose to be happy all day? What if you chose not to let anyone in authority upset your internal peace?

As difficult as it is for you to believe, you really are the chef in your kitchen of life experience. If you want to hang on to the burnt ingredients you will always have that taste in your mouth. Today is a new day. New ingredients. New menu. Pick a smile over a scowl. Pick reading a book over gossiping. Pick stretching your body over sleeping more. Pick prayer over condemnation of others.

You have soooooooooooooo many choices. Locked up or not, no one can tell you what to think - or how to feel. That is your very own universe of possibilities. ❧

THREE SECTIONS OF THIS BOOK

The first set of tools presented in the tools section - Section One, (BODY), provides a foundation for understanding and learning. Parts of the brain are explored and placed into simple concepts. If you know what is under the hood of a car it usually makes you a more informed car owner or driver. Similarly, if you know how and why your brain works, you are likely to be more successful in your quest for internal freedom.

The second set of tools is presented in Section Two, (MIND), and provides cognitive tools to bring about change in current behavior so that immediate improvement may be experienced. In this section, additional simple tools are provided which enable you to get in the driver's seat of your life.

Section Three, (SPIRIT), provides the opportunity to support expanding knowledge and to provide a roadmap to be referred to throughout life's experiences. Seeing beyond the immediate or the obvious is a powerful tool for internal freedom.

Slow down!! Focus on one tool at a time. Really learn the tool. Practice the tool. The tools described in this book are most effective if practiced over and over again. Before you simply read this book and then put it away, use it as a weekly guide. One tool per week. Take your time and really make the changes last.

Art by
JackiLyn S.

YEAH, BUT WILL IT WORK FOR ME?

The measure of your success from this material is proportional to the amount of effort that you put into it. Those individuals who go to the gym and pump a little iron every day eventually begin to wear their results. Those individuals who put away a couple dollars a day are eventually able to buy a home, car, or a vacation.

Those individuals who meditate each day will eventually accumulate a wealth of relaxation that sets them apart from their friends. Those individuals who learn and apply the concepts described in this book also reap the rewards of their efforts over time, and in subtle increments.

Words from GOGI Girl Stephanie R.

Dear Everyone, If you are at a turning point in your life and seeking out tools to make a better you, then I highly recommend the GOGI Book & application of the tools to get started. In desperation, I found myself seeking freedom from the self-imprisonment of the bonds of addiction and the behaviors that continued to take away everything I cared about in my life. I now have purpose with a direction. The second half of my life is going to be the most exciting journey I've ever been on. Thanks to God, Coach Taylor & myself.

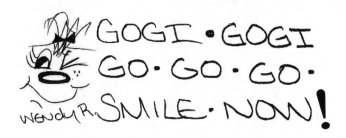

Words from Coach Taylor...

    ❧ *Change is uncomfortable, that is why many women play out the same sad scenario again and again. That is why getting and staying sober is a struggle. You know it is better for you, but it is uncomfortable and at times it feels impossible.*

    The good news is, sobriety is just a habit. Honestly. It is just a habit. And all habits – are you listening to me? – I said ALL habits can be changed.

    Get cozy with feeling uncomfortable and you will be able to change just about any habit you wish. Know and really understand that being uncomfortable is a good sign when you are breaking the habit of addiction. Really welcome feeling uncomfortable because it means you are doing something new and different.

    Get uncomfortable with new ways of thinking, speaking and acting. It means change is happening. ❧

    The tools learned each week will undoubtedly improve your life by helping you to make positive choices. When presented and incorporated into daily life, these tools will help you will gain further understanding of how those choices are made.

    Will this book work for you? This book WILL work for you – if you are ready to do the work. Again, the measure of your success is entirely proportional to the amount of effort you put into it.

    Those individuals who pick up a book for a few minutes each day will eventually accumulate a wealth of knowledge that sets them apart from their friends.

Art by Davida M.

GOGI Coach / Facilitators acknowledge the following positive attributes in everyone:

GOGI Coaches Believe...

➤ People are more good than bad.

➤ "Negative" or "bad" behavior usually stems from poor coping tools, low self-esteem, family patterns, need for attention, limited support, or misinformation.

➤ People innately want to be good, successful and to contribute positively to life and the ones they love.

➤ People sometimes lack the knowledge or support to be good, successful, or positively contribute to life.

➤ Some people get frustrated and act out when they do not get the help they need. Many individuals do not know how to ask for the help they need.

➤ People may behave poorly out of bad habits, and/or they may be frightened, disappointed, insecure, scared, angry, or do not know other ways of being.

➤ Peers are more influential teachers of behavior than academic teachers. Behaviors are more easily changed with peer support.

➤ People develop new, more productive, habits that become automatic with practice.

➤ People respond well to positive reinforcement.

➤ People's awareness of weak areas improves with an awareness of and focus on strengths.

➤ People's strengths can be utilized as tools for change.

➤ People's lives get better when honesty, trustworthiness, integrity, and honor are incorporated into their behavior.

EL REGALO MAS HERMOSO ES LA VIDA-GOGI Girl Yamileth H.
Nadie me dijo que oir ese sonido, el latido de mi Corazon.
Transformaria mi forma de pensar, durante mi vida desde el momento
que oi esos latidos. Senti que habia un ser dentro de mi. El solo pensar
en perder esta vida me era inconcevible. Respire profundo, ahora
mismo, alli donde esta Ud. En algun lugar, dentro de alguien, en este
momento quizas en alguna mujer. Esta creciendo una nueva vida y
respirara, a caso es un nuevo sentir. Una esperanza o alguien esta
respirando con dolor y dipicultad siente que la muerte esta cerca. Por
mas distintos que seamos unos de otros. Todos compartimos un regalo
en comun "La vida." Desde el momento que su existeneia comenzo
dentro de su madre hasta el momento que sus ojos se cierren en por
ultima vez. "La vida es sagrada" La vida viene de Dios; ese es su
regalo, La oportunidadpara concientizar nuestra existencia nos la
concede el unico señor de esta vida. Cualquier que sea sus
circustancias piense que siempre hay una salida. Una luz, un camino.
Gracias GOGI. Para mi...GOGI...
Genera espiritualidad elevando la dignidad de cada persona
Organizando nuestras pensamientos, acciones y sentido por la vida
Grandes resultados y cambios obtenemos cuando nos entregamos
Incondicionalmente a nuestros propositos y metas.

• • • • • • • • • • • • • •

THE MOST BEAUTIFUL GIFT ISLIFE –GOGI Girl Yamilieth H.
No one told me that at the sound of that tune. My heart beat, would
transform my way of thinking. Throughout my life from the moment I
heard those beats I felt a being inside of me. Just the thought of losing
this life is inconceivable. Take a deep breath right now, wherever you
are in a place inside yourself, right this moment. In a woman, a new
life is growing and breathing. Maybe a new feeling, a hope. Even
though we are no different from one another. We share one gift in
common. "Life." From the moment she choses her eyes for the last
time. "Life is sacred," Liife comes from God, that is His gift. The
opportunity to comply to our existence was granted by the only One of
their life: Whatever the circumstances, always think that there is a
way out. A light road. Thank you GOGI. To me GOGI is...
Generates spirituality elevating a person's dignity
Organizing our thoughts and actions and sense for life
Great result and changes we obtain when we surrender
In consideration of our purpose and goals

TOOLS FOR THE BODY

GOGI COACHES 2008

GETTING OUT BY GOING IN
COACHES 2008

Art by
Natalie H.

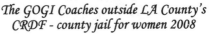

The GOGI Coaches outside LA County's
CRDF - county jail for women 2008

Words from GOGI Girl Angela B.
>   God has blessed me to find this space
>   so that he can fill that empty place.
> It's so easy to believe the bad things are true
> but when you dig deeper, you find the inner you.
>   GOGI has shown me a whole new way to live
>   life differently and watch what I say.
> The old me has to go
> so that my positive changes can always show.
>   All I know is, that true success
>   is only achieved when you've done your best.

CHAPTER 3

LET GO... FORGIVE...
& CLAIM RESPONSIBILITY

YOUR EARLY RELEASE

Many women believe that they are trapped or imprisoned — even if they are not in a physical jail or prison run by a State, or the BOP. Getting out of the prison of limited or faulty thinking can be a bigger challenge than a physical prison because it means letting go, forgiving and claiming responsibility for your life. This may cause discomfort, or it just plain hurts, but requires you to keep going if you really want to be free.

By making use of the tools in this book, you may begin to see signs of an early release from a self-imposed, solitary confinement. The signs, however, may be subtle.

You may notice a new calmness in your daily life. It may be that someone comments, "What's up with you?" or "What's going on?" or "Are you doing OK?"

It is likely that you will feel more relaxed, can sleep better, and smile a bit more. Friends or family may not understand this as positive change, and they may voice concern, criticism or even contempt. As you communicate in new ways, you are sending new messages through new actions or by non-actions. This may disturb the comfort level of those closest to you. Don't be discouraged.

If you continue on your path, you might perhaps find new and different opportunities to learn and grow, and, notice individuals and places in ways that are surprisingly refreshing.

It is likely that you will have a wider perception of your own possibilities. If this is the case, then it is the time to set goals for yourself, both personally and professionally.

You are in a powerful position for change and transformation with new tools like those that are described in this book.

DATA must be presented within enough SPACE and perceptual SHIFT for lasting CHANGE to occur. DATA (information) is presented in the materials of this book. Give yourself the time (SPACE) to let change occur through perceptual widening, or a greater understanding leading to CHANGE.

Stay consistent with the SPACE + DATA + SHIFT = CHANGE equation and you will truly experience personal mastery. Remember, you will need to sustain that CHANGE long enough to have the change become a habit in your body. The most critical part of CHANGE is sustaining it long enough so that you do not have to repeat the same process - over and over - again.

What, then, is Internal Freedom?

Words from Coach Taylor...

☙ *Internal freedom costs, but the price is worth it. It will cost you time, patience and practice, three things which are a small price for the long lasting pleasure internal freedom brings.*

☙ *Take the time to develop new habits, sober habits.*

☙ *Be patient. Grow from the inside first.*

☙ *Practice sober decisions, over and over again*

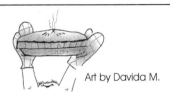

Art by Davida M.

Words from Coach Taylor...

℘ *If you are willing to change enough things in your life you will experience internal freedom. What would it be like to have internal freedom? Well, here is a preview.*

~ *When you are internally free, the behaviors of others don't bother you one bit.*

~ *When you are internally free, you are curious about the world and start to learn more, enjoying new things.*

~ *When you are internally free, you want to learn new ways of responding.*

~ *When you are internally free, you can create any new habit you wish.*

~ *When you are internally free, you choose positive friends.*

~ *When you are internally free, you do not think of using.*

~ *When you are internally free, you are happy to be alive.*

~ *When you are internally free, you are content with today, knowing that you control how you feel and what you think.*

Internal freedom is available to you, no matter where you live, your age, how much school you have. Internal freedom does not even require that you be able to read, or walk, or talk. Internal freedom comes from making choices that support a healthy and sober life.

Make a choice today, any choice, which supports your internal freedom. Make that choice then feel how it feels to support your own internal freedom. If you are still for just a moment, you will feel the glimpses of internal freedom. ℘

FACT: INTERNAL FREEDOM COSTS

Let's be brutally honest about Internal Freedom. Internal Freedom is free but it has a big price. No internal freedom comes without a price being paid. It will cost you your ego and your will, two things that individuals have a tendency to defend to the death.

If you are willing to pay the price of taking that lonesome and sometimes painful walk beyond the confines of your ego and bad habits, you will find that freedom is waiting. If you want to experience internal freedom, you will need to pay the price in three areas of your life:

1. **LET GO.** You will need to let go. This means you need to let go of resentments, pain inflicted to or from another, heartaches, and grudges.

2. **FORGIVE.** You will need to forgive yourself and all others. Close the door on the pain of the past as you focus on your internal freedom from the influences of others.

3. **RESPONSIBILITY.** You will need to assume total responsibility in your life. Stand up and be accountable. Admit your wrong actions.

Let's look at each area to see if you can identify clear ways to get yourself closer to total and complete responsibility for your thoughts and actions and subsequently, the results that you produce in your life.

LET GO

Letting go is difficult when you are not certain how far you might fall. Fear is a big obstacle. We fear what we do not know. What we fear we do not embrace. So, we repeat our failures again and again because we are fearful of what will happen to us if we change.

Individuals often remain in destructive relationships, unfulfilling occupations, or unhealthy bodies and minds due to fear of the unknown. They don't clearly see what it would be like to experience things differently.

It is easier for governments and large organizations to manipulate the masses because people generally do not want to "let go" of current ways of thinking and limit the exploration or desire to try new ways. They complain or blame. But they rarely "let go."

Most individuals do not want to "let go" of their sense of "security" even if it is detrimental it is to their life. It is easy to habitually "grab on" to more and more. Consequently, we have huge homes, huge cars, huge storage units, huge debt, huge anxiety, huge depression and a huge lack of time. How can you swim against the prevailing tide and begin to do things differently?

Inside the "laboratory" or the institution of "Higher Learning" represented by the four walls holding you in place, you have the opportunity to develop and flex the muscle of personal mastery of internal freedom.

FLEX YOUR MUSCLES

Your stay in prison is intended to be a punishment, but it is possible to use your time as a rare opportunity for your personal empowerment.

Your incarceration can be turned into an experience from many different perspectives. Your ability to flourish and thrive behind bars is entirely dependent upon the parts of incarceration that you choose to focus on.

When you let things go, you have the opportunity to work through the ugliness that inevitably surfaces. Then you will find the place where you are ultimately free — regardless of the walls that confine you.

> *Words from GOGI Girl Adrianne K.*
>
> Today I have to let go of everything. I have taken this opportunity to shed everything. I'm doing time, time is not doing me. I can't afford to fill my mind with all the stuff that I have no control over.
>
> GOGI is filling me with new thoughts. It wasn't until I completely let go that I was able to begin to fill myself up with all that GOGI has to offer. I meditate, do yoga and take all kinds of classes.
>
> I've let go and have forgiven. I'm taking responsibility. I'm also responsible for tomorrow. That's something I look forward to today...because I know that I will be free on the inside and out.

Words from GOGI Girl JackiLyn S.

For me, in order to change I must truly want to change for myself. I know I will not be scared because I will be letting go. Flexing my muscles is doing positive things. Doing my time positively -- while fighting to get the help I needed -- to learn to change myself...This isn't easy. I've been in and out of prison 18 years, and now I'm off of parole, not on probation and fighting to be free. I had to let go...let God! For me, all it take is giving back to others and giving back to society for all the wrong I've done. I now know drugs only numb my problems for a moment. By forgiving myself, I'm able to forgive others and put my past to rest.

I had to set boundaries to live my life in a sober way. I now have boundaries with persons, places and things that I know will help my life. With proper boundaries I can learn to forgive myself and others.

It was hard for me to take responsibility for all the wrong I have done. But today I accept all and I have come to terms that I am responsible for all my wrong doing. I have learned that not all money is good. Blaming others was easier than blaming myself; but by being responsible for myself, I take ownership.

Being released in jail before even being released to freedom was something new. I'm still in jail but I'm released in my inner self. Thank you GOGI Coach Taylor. I never believed I could feel this way.

We no longer need to fear but we need to feel. Sometimes we fear what we feel. We need to let Go AND let God. This is so true. We must let go and let God / forgive ourselves. For me, these tools have given me a new beginning and a freedom from old self. We must set goals for ourselves in order to grow! Thank you so much GOGI for helping me live! I can now let go and let GOD!

YOUR RARE OPPORTUNITY BEHIND BARS

We often do not like what we see in the mirror when we are absent of the trimmings that come with living. Cutting off the cuffs and freeing yourself of "stuff" is the first step in letting go. It is rare that an individual has the opportunity to LET GO and start to remake their lives from a new way of looking at living.

More often than not, this process is one that many may not experience until they are on their deathbed. That is when individuals almost always become concerned about how they treated other individuals. When forced with the reality of their mortality, they suddenly realize all their stuff is staying behind and the only things they take with them are the knowledge, experience, and love expressed along the way.

What would it take for you to truly LET GO of an attachment to "stuff"? What will it take for you to be more concerned about bringing a smile to someone instead of getting back at them for what they said, jockeying in line for food, or filing a complaint because your boss unfairly accused you of not doing your job?

Words from GOGI Girl Mary R.

For myself, my life was filled with material things that only last a season. Now, I am realizing it was never important at all. Finally, I took a look at my life and cried out to God for help. I didn't have nowhere to go.

I knew my purpose of life wasn't being met and stuff wasn't making my life whole. My family is my purpose of life. What program could help my need? One day, God will answer my prayers. I am glad I am able to experience the unique GOGI Campus created by a godsend angel Coach Taylor.

Words from GOGI Girl Charissa C.

I have never felt so sober and real in experience with GOGI. I can be honest and open about my guilt or failures. I can cry and work through my pain and find a selection of solutions, not just one, through the GOGI book & tools. Most importantly, I am not alone. I have so much support and faith from my peers and coaches.

You are not alone...

There is an increasing number of women reading and learning from the GOGI books. This, alone, means that no matter how lonely you feel, you are not alone. All over the United States there are incarcerated men, women and children who are learning the tools it takes to be a powerful force for good in our society. You have real friends.

What will it take?

What will it take for you to tell your loved ones that you are willing to LET GO of anger and begin the long journey to internal freedom, and that you need their help and support throughout the process? What will it take for you to look beyond your own myopic experience of the world around you?

Maybe you can begin to offer help to others or volunteer to assist those organizations who are helping others. Maybe you can simply help by listening more than you speak.

You can LET GO simply by taking two steps beyond the resentments, two steps beyond pain inflicted to and by another, two steps beyond the heartache and two steps beyond your grudges.

Here is what you are likely to experience if you study and master LET GO and the other techniques described in this book.

Let Go of...

- Thinking you need a drug to make you happy.
- Thinking you need a man to make you happy.
- Thinking you need to get revenge.
- Thinking you need money.
- Thinking you need a car.
- Thinking you need any THING except INTERNAL FREEDOM.
- Thinking that THINGS make you more successful, powerful, desirable.
- Thinking THINGS represent freedom.

Thinking *things* matter is a guarantee that you will not experience internal freedom. THINGS get in the way of internal freedom. THINGS are the real prison. Truly let go of THINGS and....

"Let go put your Heart Your Kids NEED You in to it. you are worth it. by GOOGI GIRL

Art by Mary R.

Words from a GOGI Girl...
I remember these simple guidelines for internal happiness.
1. Free your heart from hate.
2. Free your mind from worry
3. Live simple.
4. Give more.
5. Expect less.   - GOGI Campus Student

GOGI Girl Lisa W. and son.

Words from GOGI Girl Vicki W.
      Myself
   I have no one to blame but
myself this time, I was doing too
much and committed a crime.
   My verdict was guilty, now I'm doing
my time. I cry for my family, and 8-year-old son,
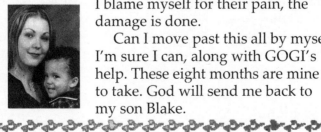
I blame myself for their pain, the
damage is done.
        Can I move past this all by myself?
I'm sure I can, along with GOGI's
help. These eight months are mine
to take. God will send me back to
my son Blake.

Truly Let Go and...

- You will smile more.
- You will breathe more fully.
- You will attract truly successful individuals.
- You will earn REAL respect.
- You will see possibilities and joy where you previously experienced darkness and despair.
- You will think of more people as likable or you may even find them fascinating.
- You will begin to experience the finest "drug" of all....Internal Freedom.

YOUR CHALLENGE - 60 MINUTES

Give yourself a challenge. Set aside one hour a day - just sixty short minutes. In those sixty minutes, make a conscious choice to use the GOGI tools to help you LET GO. Maybe it is the first hour of your day when you set your mind to focus on being the best you can be.

LET GO of all those things keeping you from being your best. LET GO of thoughts regarding your addictions and the BOP. LET GO of thoughts of your incarceration. LET GO of thoughts about your appeal. LET GO of thoughts about your remaining years behind bars. LET GO of your accusers. LET GO of everything that deters you from experiencing this day, this 60 minutes, as the best possible.

Start each day with MENTAL FREEDOM, having LET GO of the psychological chains that bind you to internal incarceration.

You may choose to say, "I will make today internally peaceful, regardless of my environment, LETTING GO of anything that stands in my way of internal freedom."

The truth is...the only one standing in the way of your internal freedom is YOU! Get out of your way! In addition to LET GO, there are other steps, none more or less challenging than the others, on your journey to Getting Out of Prison Before Your Release.

NEXT...

The second step along this journey of Getting Out of Prison Before Your Release is one of FORGIVENESS OF OURSELVES AND OTHERS.

FORGIVENESS...OF OURSELVES AND OTHERS

When we hold on to events of the past, we limit our potential for positive experiences. It goes back to the concept of holding on to extra "baggage" that we no longer need. Some people may believe that if they LET GO they will be subjected to the same type of pain, and the same experience all over again. We, as humans, automatically store our experiences in our subconscious memory, just in case we need to remember or protect ourselves from similar ones.

The brain is wonderfully efficient and logs our suffering. We remember the suffering and attempt to avoid it, but inevitably re-create it time and time again because we have a fixed focus on the suffering.

It is almost as if by NOT forgiving, we doom ourselves to remain in the cycle of re-creating the very thing we wish to avoid.

If you have a friend and he steals from you, then it is not wise to leave your wallet out in the open. That's just not smart. It is not protecting you and it may be tempting him beyond his ability to resist.

What forgiveness means is that you protect yourself through a positive and proactive perspective, not from a negative or reactionary approach. It also means that you don't leave your wallet out to tempt anyone. Consider your surroundings. You have control over where you leave your wallet.

Clearly defined boundaries

Forgiveness of yourself means that you protect yourself enough so that you do not invite experiences that require forgiveness.

Stay away from troublemakers or those whose integrity or honor is questionable. Stay true to your word and expect that others will do the same.

With established boundaries that are clearly and calmly stated, you are raising the bar of the behavior of those around you.

Having clearly defined boundaries means that you will need to forgive less often because individuals will behave differently around you.

Life doesn't frighten me...
GOGI GOGI
GOGI go go
go
Overcoming is our goal...

Words from GOGI Girl Wendy R.
Let Go, Forgive & Claim Responsibility
    I'm letting go of all my pain,
forgiving myself for not being there as a
    mother to my children, Manuel and Priscilla
whom I love so much and
    I am claiming responsibility in my life today.

~Simple Rule ~

Here are two simple rules that will never lead you in the wrong direction...
~ sober or not near me...If you make it a rule to only speak with people when they are sober it is likely you will remain sober.

If someone calls you and they are loaded tell them you will speak with them tomorrow. If someone comes over to your home and they are high, tell them to return tomorrow. Build a boundary. sober, or not near me. ~ sober or I am outta here...

If you make it a rule to only be in the room with people who are sober, it is likely you will remain sober.

Art by Dora B. D.

If you go somewhere and someone is not sober, turn and head out the door. Build a boundary. sober or I am outta here.

If you follow these two rules it is likely you will be happier and more successful than you could ever imagine.♥Coach Taylor

Walking beyond your past

FORGIVENESS means walking beyond past negative experiences and strengthening yourself internally so that you are aware and prepared to avoid such experiences in the future.

FORGIVENESS requires you to LET GO.

LET GO and the art of FORGIVENESS of self and others work well with each other.

CONSIDER THIS...

Tonight, as the lights go out and you are left with your thoughts, consider what it would be like to live completely free of memories that might require your forgiveness.

What would you feel like if you had nothing or no one to forgive? How would you sleep if there were nothing in your life to forgive? What would your day be like tomorrow if you had nothing more to forgive?

If you are willing to be free, truly free, you will let go and forgive. As you drift off to sleep, let your subconscious mind muse at the possibility of releasing ill feelings toward yourself and others.

In releasing these thoughts and feelings, you are empowered to move beyond the confines, the "prison," of holding on.

ASSUME TOTAL RESPONSIBILITY

The final step toward Getting Out of Prison Before Your Release is to accept total responsibly for your life. Total responsibly permits you to claim ownership of your life. Total responsibility puts you in control of the events of your life.

Someone may ask, "Are you saying I caused my father to beat me?" or "You mean I am responsible for the poverty I was born into?" It would surely be extremely naive, even disrespectful to claim that another individual is the cause of misfortune or abuse that comes your way. This is not the case. If your father beat you, or you were born into poverty, however, it does not give you the right or the excuse to be anything less than a wonderful and peaceful human being.

REACTIONS DEFINE YOU

There are countless autobiographies and biographies of individuals of every culture, race, creed, color, religion and who raise themselves from "rags to riches", moving beyond the confines of their childhood into powerful positions within their communities.

Believe it or not, your life, regardless of the darkness of its history, may be molded and shaped by you to reflect a "rags to riches" scenario of internal accomplishments. Your "dark" history can be the key to your bright future.

It is not easy to be a REAL success. It takes determination and dedication. It takes an unwavering dedication. It takes letting go of every THING that gets in the way of your freedom. Let it go. It is not worth it. Easy money is not worth it.

Easy money is cheap, lazy, false, fake, and disappears as soon as the Feds break down the door and yell "FREEZE!" Go for the REAL gold - the gold that comes from INTERNAL FREEDOM. Let THAT shine.

You are responsible

The fact is: you are totally RESPONSIBLE for your REACTIONS. Your REACTIONS to things, events, places and people are your RESPONSIBILITY.

In a very real way, your reactions create your reality. Your perceptions affect your level of responsibility and your reactions. How you think about an event determines your reaction. What happens to your physical body may be up to God, Allah, Buddha, Fate, Karma or bad luck of the draw. How you REACT to what happens is totally and completely YOUR RESPONSIBILITY.

When you ASSUME TOTAL RESPONSIBILITY, you move into the most powerful position that any individual can experience. You become a creator of your experience. Pick and choose those things that you endorse as desirable and steer clear of those things that do not serve you.

Stop blaming others…

Countless inmates blame the system, staff, warden, buddies, wives, co-defendants, witnesses, DA, the government, or environment for their internal condition. When you blame someone else for anything, you re-create negative thoughts within your mind.

You are feeding your mind with negative thoughts when you say, "If the warden were not such a…." or "If she would only…" or "If I were not locked up, then I would not be depressed…" or "How can I not be angry, you have no idea what I am going through!"

Negative thoughts keep you stuck in the web of "their" control. Get out of their web. Walk away from the negative thoughts.

Changes occur when an inmate decides to LET GO, FORGIVE and ASSUME TOTAL RESPONSIBILITY. Their face brightens. A smile replaces a frown. Posture straightens and they select words differently. Good things begin to happen to them. Somehow, the world seems to be a better place when these people are nearby.

Words from GOGI Girl Wendy L.

Wanting it Bad Enough to "Change." I knew the GOGI tools were working when I finally let go of all the old baggage. I forgave myself and others for the wrong doings and pain that has been eating me up inside.

I knew the tools were working when I started taking total responsibility for my actions and reactions. I really wanted to be given a drug program rather than go to prison.

Then I finally accepted and understood fully that it didn't matter where I was going to get sober and stay sober. If I wanted it bad enough, I could do it in a cell, by the beach, in the Hamptons (ha, ha), etc.

That's what letting go, forgiving, and taking responsibility means to me.

Art by Taylor M.

GETTING OUT OF PRISON BEFORE YOUR RELEASE

Getting Out of Prison Before Your Release is FREE but it comes at a cost. Countless individuals have paid that price. And as difficult as it is, as frightening as the journey may seem to be, as daunting of a task as it appears, no one regrets their decision to:

- LET GO
- FORGIVE
- CLAIM RESPONSIBILITY

The path to INTERNAL FREEDOM and GETTING OUT OF PRISON BEFORE YOUR RELEASE takes you through the process of Letting Go, Forgiveness and Assuming Total Responsibility for Your Life.

More than thirty percent of inmates never return to prison. That represents many individuals who decided to change their lives. By making the decision to change your life, you can be one of those people and help reduce recidivism. Consider teaching your Bunkie, as well. With enough women learning to LET GO, FORGIVE and CLAIM RESPONSIBILITY, the INMATES can even make prisons obsolete.

Traditional religions, ancient spiritual cultures and spiritual practices such as yoga and meditation attempt to nudge you in the direction of internal peace. The concepts of LET GO, FORGIVE and claiming TOTAL RESPONSIBILITY are a part of these practices, as well as being universal. Tools of internal freedom are taught in many different forms with many different names.

The GOGI approach and the techniques herein attempt to provide you with enough DATA to create enough internal SPACE to support SHIFT and the inevitable CHANGE that occurs.

> ✇ *We either live a life where we choose how we react or we abdicate our power and let life live us, permitting others & situations to determine our destiny. At every moment of every day we are either living our life or letting our life live us.* ✇
>
> *Coach Taylor*

Words from GOGI Girl Lili R.

The following poem was written by a GOGI Girl. Missing her daughters, she expressed her love for them in poem. Nearly 80 percent of incarcerated women are mothers. Their children are shuffled off into the system off to over-burdened family members.

My Little Angels

My little angels that were Heaven sent
You are probably wondering where Mommy went.
She doesn't call and doesn't show.
What's going on, you want to know.
I've gone away for a little while
Girls, don't cry and give me a smile.
God will protect you and he has a plan
Just reach out to Him and give Him your hand.
He will make you strong and make you brave
And listen to you both, whenever you pray.
So don't feel lonely and don't be mad.
Just look up to Heaven when you are sad.
And every time you think of me
Remember God has set me free.
He's made me strong and given me joy
That no one can take or ever destroy.
So pray to God to bring us together
And I promise you happiness to last forever.

Words from GOGI Girl Felicia (Mimi) J.

Self-Awareness

My Early release...Wow!!! What a concept. One that really touch my inner secret heart. I am a 43 year African American woman who has been afflicted with the bondage of drugs and alcohol. I have been in and out of every female prison in California for the past 25 years. I am now writing this message from inside a County facility.

GOGI - Getting Out by Going In, has afforded me the opportunity to let go, forgive and claim responsibility which sounds like an old cliché, but in all actuality has given me my early release.

In this chapter, I read about getting out of the prison in my mind. I have come to notice within myself the joy of catching a new calmness in my character. It's such a trippy experience that others in my module ask me, "Are you o.k., what is going on with you?" I tend to just smile because I know that in my other circumstance, I would have been the instigator, the one yelling and causing the ruckus. And for those who know me, they wonder what is going on with Felicia. I am finding new ways to communicate and a new way of thinking. I'm loving every minute of it. I am free. But again, it takes what it takes. Letting go is a very humbling experience. I've grown accustomed to staying angry and upset with the individual who betrayed me, who stole from me and slept with my boyfriend. That frame of mind was touchy and had a large ego.

Cont. next page

Words from GOGI Girl Felicia (Mimi) J. Continued

'Who do you think you are doing that to me! I am going to get you; and I have to let everyone else know that I am going to get you because IF I DON'T, I WILL BE CONSIDERED 'THE PUNK,' I don't think so.

So, beginning to embrace or even think about this change hurt to the core. I then took it a step further. Everyone with whom I was upset was not coming to jail, was not losing their jobs, was not losing their kids to the system. Something here just ain't right.

I am embracing new and different opportunities to learn and grow because I am tired of falling behind. Remember, for some it takes what it takes and I made a conscious decision to give myself time (SPACE), to let change occur through opening the tools of this book in my mind or as the books says, a greater understanding leading to CHANGE.

Staying consistent with the SPACE + DATA (information given) + SHIFT = CHANGE. Since I have some time on my hands, why not stay consistent & give myself a break today and utilize this stability. If I stay focused on being focused, something's got to break.

The most critical part of CHANGE is sustaining it long enough so that you do not have to repeat the same process over and over again.

Letting go is very difficult because I do not know what to expect, or what the outcome will be. The unknown is scary, especially if I'm used to doing it my way. I have trust issues.

Cont. next page

Words from GOGI Girl Felicia (Mimi) J. Continued

To jump out with blind trust on circumstances as important as YOUR LIFE is very scary. FEAR (there goes that word again) is the greatest obstacle - it's like having nothing to fear but fear itself. So because I'm not trying to experience a great let down of the ego, pride and whatever else. I hold on and repeat coming back to jail, repeat using again even though I may have experienced a brief session of how drugs aren't good for me; they're not working for me anymore. Can you understand?

This is my rare opportunity behind bars. And I hear what you are saying and I want it. Not that I need it because my mom tells me that I need it, my boyfriend tells me that I need it, the judge tells me that I need it and guess what, it's not that I need it, I WANT IT!!

What will it take? For me it took 25 years of pure misery in the midst of my thinking I was happy. Go figure. Don't let it take 25 years for you. Truly letting go is smiling more, breathing more effectively, attracting successful individuals, earning REAL respect, experiencing true inner joy, liking people you didn't care for anyone, and you, as will I, experience the finest drug of all... INTERNAL FREEDOM.

Note: Thanks to the tools of this chapter I have learned to begin to take responsibility of my actions, stop blaming others, become accountable, establish sound boundaries, embrace the wreckage of my past (amends), and move forward. I am looking forward to the new me, and GOGI...Thank You!!

Words from GOGI Girl Shekinah L.
No longer helpless
As I take a glance at the past sometimes,
now it's clear to read between the lines
As I make the changes I need to
I move from the pain of you…
Yeah, you constantly cheated and lied
Didn't care how many times I cried
But this one good thing I learned from you
A person can only do to me what
I allow them to.
I no longer feel helpless now and I Know…
It's time for me to change
And it's a long road but I've let go
Now I've moved on…
All the things I've ever done I'd never change
There is always sunshine after rain
As you can see I didn't wither in the storm
And no one will ever again leave me torn
My broken wings are fixed now I can Fly
And you can see me moving into light
And now I feel so happy about me!
And finally my shackle and chains are free.
I no longer feel helpless now cuz I know
Things will never be the same
Now I moved on and I'm strong,
The lights are on.
i no longer feel helpless now and I know.
My life's moved into a positive change,
It's a long road I've let go
Now I've moved on.

Words from GOGI Girl Andrea W.
SPACE + DATA + SHIFT = CHANGE

S – Being sure of myself today.

P – Being at peace with who I am & where I come from.

A – Accepting life on life terms today. Willing to make change.

C – Courage to change and the Confidence in knowing I can make a difference.

E – Being able to encourage others & give enlightenment to those that want the same kind of change.

D – Start disciplining our minds, bodies, and souls & start dedicating ourselves to new tools and goals.

A – We have to change our attitudes on a day-to-day basis.

T – Trust Me! GOGI tools work for all ages.

A – Action. Start putting GOGI tools into action.

S – Sharing your experience with others.

H – Be honest with yourself and others.

I – You don't have to be intelligent to make better choices.

F – Forgive yourself and others.

T – Turn your life around with the support of GOGI and GOGI coaches

CHANGE: Change is something only you can do by being willing and surrendering to being honest with yourself. It is a desire that comes from your heart. Take that first step and put it into action

Can we change? Yes, we can change. Start by the way you think. If you think you are a winner, then become a winner! Start changing the way you act. Dismiss your "I don't care" about me, to "I do care about what happens." Begin cleaning out all the garbage you have kept locked inside your mind.

CHAPTER 4

BOSS OF YOUR BRAIN

The powerful tool you will soon have in the journey to internal freedom is knowledge; knowledge about your physical body. **When you gain knowledge about any subject you have the ability to improve and direct ideas, thoughts and actions.**

When someone learns about the parts of the car under the hood, they become a more informed driver. An informed driver has the opportunity to become a better driver. I bet you were a better drug addict when you knew how to find the drugs. Similarly, if you learn how to find the power inside your brain you will make better decisions.

In this chapter, you will be given permission to look under the "hood of your car." You will learn just a little bit about how your brain functions. If you know more you will be able to choose more wisely. Through this knowledge, you will have the opportunity to become BOSS OF YOUR BRAIN.

Focus on and practice the concept presented in this chapter. It is very important to truly understand your power. If you skip a few days - make them up and repeat the reading again and again and again. Take notes. Reading your notes again and again will permit you to track your own internal progress. Really, really understand and come to believe you are the Boss!

CREATE YOUR OWN COLLEGE

College students are taught the value of making study notes in notebooks or the margins of books. They are no smarter than you. They just learned that taking notes is helpful.

"THE BOSS OF WHAT?"
- by Jennifer B.

Someone took the time to teach them how to take notes. Well, now you have no more excuses. You have learned that note taking empowers you.

Don't worry about spelling correctly. The notes are for your eyes only. It is your book. Mark it up as much as you want. The fact is that taking notes empowers you to learn more.

Be like a successful college student and take notes. Read any book over and over again and you will learn new things by reflecting on your notes in the margins. Now that you know that taking notes can be helpful, you can put into practice something that has helped college students for centuries.

Make notes about what you read, reflect on your learning and incorporate what you read into your daily thoughts. Move to the next chapter only when you are confident that you have integrated and added the previous learning to your toolbox of change.

Give yourself time for the process of change to unfold. If this book sits by your bed for a couple of months, just open one page and read it moments before lights out. Glance over your notes and reflect on the process of change. Thirty seconds of nightly reflection, when added over the weeks and months, brings immeasurable results. Even if it is only thirty seconds of reading — having positive and helpful information nearby can offer great support.

Most importantly, remember that change takes time. Please do yourself a favor and let the process of change unfold naturally. Make time to practice each tool so you may experience the positive changes that others found possible with these simple tools.

LET'S GET STARTED

Many women believe that their brain is not controllable. They believe their brain controls them. "It's just the way I am," often becomes the automatic response when life gets out of control. This is simply not true.

Your brain operates much like a car. You can drive it wherever you want to, but if you take your hands off the wheel, the car might spin out of control or go in another direction. Your brain is yours to change, mold and shape to do exactly what you want it to do.

Simply put, you (and only you) are the **BOSS OF YOUR BRAIN**.

Difficulty in controlling your actions or thoughts stems from not understanding your personal abilities and powers, and from neglecting your right to create desired thoughts or behavior.

As you learn how the brain functions, you are likely to make an effort to control your thoughts rather than to buy into the concept of "it's just the way I am."

Words from GOGI Girl Mary R.
There are a lot of advantages being the BOSS of your BRAIN.
Reclaim your dream's reach for the moon and aim for the stars.
GOGI has the tools. Let's get started.

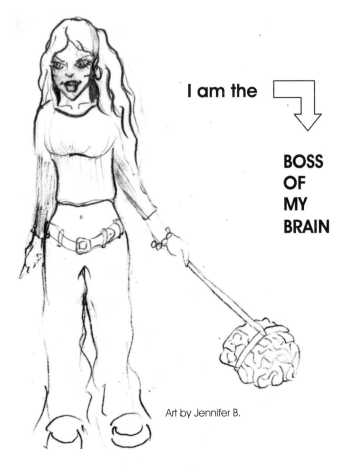

I am the

BOSS
OF
MY
BRAIN

Art by Jennifer B.

Learning the basics about how your brain functions is like learning to drive. For example, consider when a 16-year-old learns how a car works. By learning to operate the vehicle with increasing skill and efficiency, he/she is able to keep the vehicle on the road and inside the designated lanes.

Compare how you control, alter, modify and change your brain to when you are behind the wheel of a car. It may not always seem like it, but you truly have control of the vehicle called your body and your brain.

Your brain is yours to command, to direct, to steer in the direction that you, and only you, dictate. You are in the driver's seat. No one else is driving your car. **You** are behind the wheel — not the warden, not the guard, not your Bunkie. You are the only one in control of your reactions, your thoughts and your words. Therefore, only you control your future. You and only you are the BOSS OF YOUR BRAIN.

Art by Taylor M.

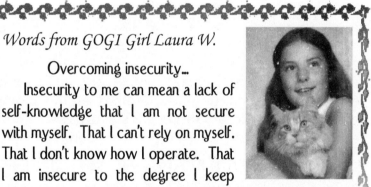

Words from GOGI Girl Laura W.

Overcoming insecurity...

Insecurity to me can mean a lack of self-knowledge that I am not secure with myself. That I can't rely on myself. That I don't know how I operate. That I am insecure to the degree I keep parts of myself hidden from myself. Or insecurity can mean I know how I operate but don't think it's good enough.

When I find myself trying to figure out beforehand how I should act (that is planning it out) this shows me I lack respect for the way I am. I can't be trusted to be perfect and so I have to make rules.

Otherwise, I just might slip and be a human being.

COMFORT

Women, and men, often find a comfort zone within their bad habits. This comfort zone leads them to believe that their reactions and thoughts are beyond their control. More frequently than not, men and women who are incarcerated individuals have a lengthy list of bad habits that have perpetuated the same unproductive behavior over and over.

No one wants to be a slave to drugs and crime; they just haven't learned the tricks to taking control. It is likely that recidivism rates would drop significantly if individuals understood and practiced being in control of their brain.

How can a 16-year-old drive across the country if no one told them what is under the hood of the car, or how to read a road map? It is almost impossible to drive very far without a map, or "DATA." Although the internal nitro-fueled mental "engine" of your brain may be under-nourished or under-utilized at the moment, you can still be the **BOSS OF YOUR BRAIN.** You can begin making modifications right now. Today.

The **BOSS OF YOUR BRAIN** awareness will help you:

1. Take control of the way your brain processes **information**.

2. Take control of the way your brain processes **emotions**.

3. Take control of the way your brain processes **beliefs**.

Art by Davida M.

> ### THE TRUTH IS. . .
> *Being the* **BOSS OF YOUR BRAIN**
> *will allow you to make choices that are entirely yours;*
> *not society's choices, not your situation's*
> *choices not your parents' choices.*
> *Being the* **BOSS OF YOUR BRAIN**
> *will allow you to make solid decisions based on more*
> *information, wider perception, and less reaction.*

Art by Davida M.

HOW DOES <u>BOSS OF YOUR BRAIN</u> WORK?

Let's break it down in its most simple form. You need to know three parts of your brain. The front part, behind your forehead, is where your LOGICAL/SMART THINKING occurs. People who study the brain call it the EXECUTIVE FUNCTIONING area. We are going to call it the SMART THINKING area. SMART THINKING occurs is at the front of the head, just behind the forehead.

The second part that you need to know is in the very center of the brain called the LIMBIC SYSTEM where emotions are processed and assigned to thoughts. We are going to call this the EMOTIONAL CONTROL CENTER. This is where we make judgments and attach feelings to things that happen.

The third area of the brain you need to know to be the BOSS OF YOUR BRAIN is the back part of your brain that we will call the AUTOMATIC THINKING area. In this back part of your brain you store both good and bad habits. Knowledge of these three parts of the brain empowers you to be the BOSS OF YOUR BRAIN.

1) SMART THINKING – Smart thinking occurs right behind the forehead.
2) EMOTIONAL CONTROL CENTER – This starts in the very center of the brain.
3) AUTOMATIC THINKING – Old habits are stored in the back of the brain.

WHY THE BOSS OF YOUR BRAIN WORKS

Would you start a car, put your foot on the gas, take your hands off the steering wheel, and let the car go wherever it wanted? Certainly not. But this is what you do when you do not claim your right to be the **BOSS OF YOUR BRAIN**.

Being the **BOSS OF YOUR BRAIN** works because when you know you are focusing on SMART THINKING, AUTOMATIC THINKING or EMOTIONAL THINKING you are empowered to be the BOSS OF YOUR BRAIN.

When you know that parts of your brain respond a certain way, you will not permit the actions of a corrections officer to control you. You will not take your hands off the steering wheel of your life and let your car run over a cliff when a guard acts inappropriately or when your bunkie gets on your nerves.

Being the BOSS OF YOUR BRAIN allows you to drive your own car. Don't let someone else get behind the wheel and start controlling your ideas, thoughts or actions. Knowing what part of your brain is working enables you to remain in control. ◄ ♦ ►

NEURONS AND NEURO-TRANSMITTERS

Like the electrical wiring in a house or stereo, your body has a communication network that moves energy or messages from one cell of your body to the other.

In a house, a current of energy is sent from the electric pole, to the house, then to the plug or the light switch. In the human body, information is sent from one end of the neurological communication network (the center of the brain, for example) to another.

Words from GOGI Girl Aura A.
GOGI has taught me to love myself. I've found inner freedom and I've learned to be the BOSS OF MY BRAIN.
I'm making the best out of a bad situation. I'm grateful for being able to have contact visits with my two year old daughter.

Because of this network, your mouth responds with words, your hands respond in action, and your feet respond in movement, etc. Much like tracing the fuel line of a car or the wiring of a home, your body's "wiring" can be traced.

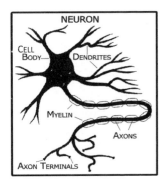

Here are the parts of your body's communication network.

• **Neuron** - A neuron is a message holder inside your body. It is squiggly and kind of looks like an octopus with tentacles – called "dendrites" – at the ends. There are billions of these octopus-like neurons in every area of your body just waiting to deliver messages to neighboring neurons all lined up anxious to receive messages telling them what you want them to do.

One neuron sends its message to another neuron ready to receive the message. Much like a river, the message flows through your body from one neuron to the next. These neurons form a web of communication, much like a spider web of connections, with messages being transmitted from a long line of dendrite endings to other dendrite endings across what is called the synaptic cleft.

• **Neurotransmitters** - Neurotransmitters are the delivery service that takes the message from one neuron to the next. Scientists call them neurotransmitters—since they are transmitters of neural messages. Think of it this way, neurons and neurotransmitters are floating down the river on an inner tube. The neurotransmitter would be the water flowing down the river. The person on the inner tube would be the message floating down the worn pathway. There are many types of neurotransmitters just like there are many different types of oil for automobiles and many different kinds of automobiles, trains or planes to move people around.

Words from GOGI Girl Laura A.

Be the Boss of Your Brain! I have learned powerful decision making tools that will forever change how I react to situations that have been aiding my addictions for years.

We are all smart people, so why not start to use smart thinking? My automatic thinking seems to think "I was just born that way." But being Boss of My Brain has taught me to take control of my thoughts and my decisions to make me a new person. Yeah!

• **Neurological Pathways** - Neurological pathways are like rivers or roads running throughout your body. Some rivers and roads are traveled over and over again. Some rivers dry up from lack of use, or form a Grand Canyon-like valley within your body because the water flows continually and runs over the same area for years and years. A neurological pathway is a sequence of neurons that sends messages to the same neurons over and over again, much like a river sending water down the same path. This pattern is repeated so much that it becomes a well-worn path through the human mind and body. It is a regular pathway of communication, a habit that you do automatically.

Words from GOGI Girl Davida M.

I will remember that date forever as my demarcation date. I'm clean and sober today (90 days). The best part of my life is ahead of me because I am finally free on the inside. What an incredible feeling to feel good enough about me to now share my knowledge and experience to support others to make their journeys become a reality for them so that we women can return to society and resume our roles as mothers, daughters and career women, out of jail and internally free. Thanks to GOGI, my spirit has been returned to allow me to be a woman with the ability to shine beyond the walls and through the clouds forever.

Since I was accepted to GOGI Campus, my life gets better every day. Today, I have my sobriety, my GOGI tools, I am in touch with my feelings. I am aware of my surroundings. I'm truly alive. Music sounds beautiful. Colors are vivid. I value myself and others. I have integrity. So this is what internal freedom feels like…No wonder I'm smiling ☺ I thank God, I thank GOGI and I thank Coach Taylor for making this possibility a reality to me. I'm alive and free.

• • • • • • • • • • •

Since requesting to become a student at GOGI Campus in CRDF in Lynwood and being fortunate enough to be accepted (less than 1:100 chance). I have emerged from the darkness of my drug addiction to take hold of responsibility for my every action. Since implementing the "GOGI tools," along with the guidance and support of Coach Taylor, her team of coaches and my peer coaches, I have learned forgiveness of myself and others, the act of "letting go" and stepping up to the plate, being accountable for my actions instead of in denial of my self-destructive behavior. By turning my past mistakes into learning experiences, I have become a woman of integrity. As I use my tool of positive T.W.A. (Thoughts, Words, Actions) from the GOGI textbook, I have formed new neurological pathways resulting in positive habits empowering me enough to advance to the 10th level of the GOGI curriculum. I was very proud to receive my certificate, I passed the exam required to become a GOGI peer coach on my 46th birthday! -DM.

Your Body's Rivers of Communication

Your body has old, worn and unproductive neurological pathways that you use when you let your brain be the boss of you. They are like worn rivers and show up as habits and behaviors that you think you have no control over.

However, when you decide that you are the BOSS OF YOUR BRAIN your body can create new, powerful and productive neurological pathways, regardless of your age, size, shape, color, religion, sex, or intelligence.

The fact is that you can build new neurological pathways any time you wish, at any age. Instead of letting the AUTOMATIC THINKING part of your brain take you into old habits, you can – I promise you – you CAN build new and improved habits if you use the front part of your brain, your SMART THINKING part.

Every individual can make new neurological pathways. When you let your mind to be the boss of itself, the neurons and neurotransmitters repeat old thoughts, old behaviors, and old ways of being, and you feel as if you have no control over your actions or thoughts. You are AUTOMATIC THINKING - replaying old habits stored in the back of your brain.

However, even though bad habits allow your body to be the boss—you can take over at any time. You and only you can become the BOSS OF YOUR BRAIN. When you are the BOSS OF YOUR BRAIN, you choose where the neurons send their messages.

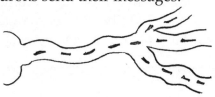

HOW TO BECOME THE BOSS OF YOUR BRAIN

Here's the process…

STEP 1) **INFORMATION IN** - This process is physiologically complex, but to keep it simple let's assume that all information comes into the very center of your brain for processing through your sense of sight, smell, touch, hearing and taste. It comes in and finds its way to the EMOTIONAL CONTROL CENTER. This is where it is assigned meaning. A judgment is made. It's good. It's bad. You can form an opinion.

STEP 2) **ELECTRICAL CURRENT** - Much like an electrical current taking power from a light switch to a bulb, this information shoots their information through your body with a meaning attached. You decide what things are, and what they mean based on previous experiences and goals. The current takes this to every cell of your body.

STEP 3) **AUTOMATIC THINKING** – When your old habits begin to AUTOMATICALLY take over, you need to get the thought back to the SMART THINKING AREA, in the front of your brain.

STEP 4) **INSERT A WEDGE** - You can cut the current of old meaning, actually re-route the neurons by sending thoughts to your SMART THINKING area, the front of your brain. Getting the thought up to the front creates a neurological WEDGE. This "wedge," or the rerouting of information, could possibly buy you just enough time to avoid many of the automatic mistakes. Your mistakes are likely to be old neurological habits that are tucked in the back of your brain.

WEDGE?

Breathing can be considered a wedge. Walking the yard may be a wedge. Speaking to a Chaplain may be a wedge. Meditating may be a wedge. Prayer may be a wedge. Writing may be a wedge. Reading may be a wedge. Whatever you do, take the thought out of the AUTOMATIC THINKING part of your brain and get it up front, behind your forehead, to your SMART THINKING area.

> *Words from GOGI Girl Charissa C.*
>
> I've found that using a wedge has saved me from many unnecessary disagreements that eventually die down and are forgotten about the very next day anyway.
>
> To notice that my wedge, which is yoga, has actually worked gives me so much peace and encouragement.

21 DAYS – ADDICTIONS BE GONE - A majority of the prisoners behind bars in America are more addicts than they are criminals. They are addicts who commit crimes to supply their addictions. What would happen if every prison taught prisoners how to break addictions by using BOSS OF YOUR BRAIN as a tool? What would happen if you broke YOUR addictions by taking your addictive thoughts out of the AUTOMATIC THINKING area for 21 days and you really focused on SMART THINKING for 21 days?

Words from GOGI Girl Kimberly P.
Like wolves, humans live in families. Like humans, wolves need friends. People display a high degree of intelligence, expressiveness and other characteristics that enable them to maintain sophisticated, family-based social bonds.

Without friends looking out for them, these families will be broken apart. But, with the help of this book, people get a better understanding of who they are.

Do you realize that if you drink a glass of water rather than light up a cigarette for 21 days, it is likely that you will have a new habit of drinking water instead of rushing to a cigarette? It's true. Try it. If you build and support a new neurological habit long enough then meth, coke, chronic, cigarettes, or cell-made wine has no power over you....none at all. You re-wire your brain to NOT INCLUDE the neurology of the old habit. When you get a new job it usually takes about 21 days before the tasks become automatic. Tasks move from the front part of your brain, SMART THINKING, to the AUTOMATIC THINKING part of your brain. Work becomes easier.

It takes about 21 days for your body's neurology to build a habit. The exciting fact is that **you may start to re-wire your body's habits today.** This can vary depending on your body's unique operating system and the subject of the new information.

It takes about 21 days for your body to replace an old habit and make a new neurological habit. Run your new neurological habit for 21 days and it will become your new neurological river. Stay away from old traps, fortify the new neurology, and stay in SMART THINKING. It will be easier to stay out of trouble.

YOU WIN!!!! NEW POSITIVE HABIT FORMED!!!

When you support a new habit of putting a wedge into the old neurological pathway for 21 days, it is likely that you will have given birth to a new, more powerful habit.

If you get thoughts out of the AUTOMATIC THINKING and into the SMART THINKING area consistently for 21 days, it is likely that you will have a new way of automatically reacting which serves you better.

TAKE TIME TO REFLECT

What are some good neurological habits that you have developed during your life? Did you know that learning to write or read is done through a neurological pathway? Learning to run, talk, react, love, or fight are all learned neurological pathways. What neurological habits have you modified while incarcerated?

Awakening at a different time or doing a new job is a new neurological pathway. What neurological habits did you change as you grew from a tiny tot to a young person and then into adulthood? We all have good and bad habits that are actual neurological pathways in our bodies. Behaviors that promote smiles in others tend to be supported by good neurological pathways. Behaviors that cause frowns, anger or withdrawal from others are likely to be pathways that you might consider reconstructing.

The truth is, it is likely that you have more GOOD and POSITIVE neurological pathways than bad ones. The problem is that the bad ones, the AUTOMATIC HABITS that get you in trouble usually are given too much control.

Signs of "good" neurological habits or traits include having a sense of humor, a good work ethic, honesty, kindness, love of family, as well as having the ability to pray, or be athletic. Good neurological pathways support growth and positive emotions. We all are born with a set of good neurological habits. Over time, we develop less productive neurological pathways. Typically, we develop poor neurological pathways as coping tools that are used to deal with situations that appear beyond our control.

All the positive abilities that you have developed are represented within your body as desirable neurological pathways. Reflect on your good and bad neurological habits. Take a few moments to assess how much of your behavior causes or creates smiles in others. How much of your behavior causes or creates irritation or negative reactions from others? How much of your behavior permits you to smile? How much of your behavior results in positive reactions from others?

Addiction, irrational anger and self-centered attitudes are all negative, unproductive neurological habits. In contrast, integrity, calmness, honesty, honor, freedom from addiction, and patience are examples of good neurological habits.

Remember, every individual has the capability to create new neurological habits. It takes about 21 days of repetitive thoughts and actions to create a new neurological habit inside your body. Take a moment and think about your own internal wiring. What are some of the neurological habits that you would like to transform? Do you like to write notes in letters or a journal? You can track your internal changes by documenting your good and bad habits.

For many women, writing is a creative process that helps synthesize information and experiences. If you wrote down your good habits and bad habits, what would you write? Would you share this list? Perhaps now is the time to begin your observation — not just of your internal world, but also the world around you.

OBSERVE OTHERS

Observation of others gives you vital information about your environment and places you in a powerful position of accepting and receiving additional knowledge or information. Observe and consider why someone behaves destructively. You can observe and use the information learned to help improve your own behavior.

Understanding the behavior and actions of others enables you to control your reactions and environment. As an added benefit, your observation allows you to react more effectively. You can learn patterns of behavior by observing others around you. Being able to predict the behavior of another is a powerful tool for your success.

Understanding the concept "I am the BOSS of MY BRAIN" gives you control in this physical environment where others are in control of what you do and where you go. When observing others, you can see that neurological pathways play out in predictable ways.

When you observe others, you are also subconsciously and automatically measuring yourself and your own options for behavior. When you observe, you may consider adding the information gleaned from the success and failure of others.

Would you handle the situation in the same manner? Would you react differently? Why is that person reacting in that way?

The Assigned Meaning

Along with my team of coaches, I volunteered at an elementary school in Watts, California. I taught children GOGI techniques to help them make stronger life choices in the future. One day when I was on the playground with the kids, I heard what I thought was a car backfiring.

"Let's go over there," one of the fifth grade boys suggested, pointing to a thick block wall dividing the playground from the street.

"Why?" I asked, naively.

"They be shooting. We are safer there," he replied.

Because my prior experience filtered the noise as a car backfire, I did not experience the sound in the same manner as the Watts-raised boy. He had heard many gunshots in his life, so his first thought was not of a car backfiring, but that we should take care to protect ourselves.

The kids and I continued our lesson next to the red brick wall; learning BOSS OF YOUR BRAIN, BELLY BREATHING, FIVE SECOND LIGHTSWITCH, WHAT IF?, POSITIVE TWA, and REALITY CHECK and other tools to empower these kids to take control of their lives.

I never learned if it was a gunshot or an automotive glitch, but that is not the point. The point is that we all have unique ways of filtering information and it is almost always based on prior experiences.

When we realize that our beliefs are based, rightly or wrongly, on prior experiences, we have the opportunity to re-think and re-wire our future experiences.

I will not hear a car backfire in the same manner, and am forever altered by my willingness to listen to another human's interpretation.

---Coach Taylor

> *CONSIDER THIS...*
> *BOSS OF YOUR BRAIN*
> is an easy tool for you to use when you need
> to take complete control of your thoughts.
> *And...BOSS OF YOUR BRAIN*
> helps oxygen get to your muscles so your body relaxes.
> A relaxed body usually makes better decisions.

Heightened awareness

There are as many different ways of reacting as there are circumstances. Some women have short fuses. Why? What provokes them? Notice when they let go of the steering wheel of their life. Do they blame the other driver for their car wreck?

"He made me!" or "It's his fault," are statements when a person takes their hands off the wheel, letting outside forces drive their life. When you observe others let go of their steering wheel, ask yourself, "Are they the Boss of their Brain or is their brain processing old, thought-less patterns?" More often than not, when reactions are angry, loud, aggressive, or out of control -- they are not the boss of their brain. They are stuck in AUTOMATIC THINKING.

Art by GOGI Girl Lilian R.

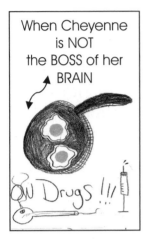

Art by Cheyenne L.

Art by Taylor W.

BOSS OF YOUR BRAIN
In Action

LILIAN STOPS YELLING

When Lilian was a kid, her parents were constantly yelling at each other, at her, at the television or anything that was not meeting their expectations. As a result, Lilian learned that she needed to yell loudly to be heard.

Over time, her body developed a neurological habit of yelling which got her into trouble at school, with friends, and she was fired from work more than once. Eventually, her yelling escalated to assault and resisting arrest—a situation that could have easily been avoided.

"It's their fault!"
by Jennifer B.

Lilian wanted, and needed, to change. She finally decided to take control of her behavior. She learned to control herself by following the BOSS OF YOUR BRAIN steps.

She practiced this tool of thinking about the wiring of her thoughts several times every day. Sometimes she slipped (relapsed) and reverted back to old neurological habits. But through constant practice, she was also beginning to strengthen a new way to respond. How did Lilian learn to be the BOSS OF HER BRAIN?

BOSS OF YOUR BRAIN IN ACTION

STEP 1)   INFORMATION IN - Lilian's boyfriend tells her that he is going out with his friends to a bar instead of seeing her. This information gets transmitted from Lilian's ears to the center of her brain. She automatically goes into her predictable response, her AUTOMATIC THINKING. A switch along the old neurological pathway gets flipped on, and sends information down the old, worn and unproductive road of yelling.

STEP 2)   ELECTRICAL CURRENT – She knows that her response to him right now is not SMART THINKING; it is a habit, an old habit. She has been down this road. Every time this happens, she starts to yell and then she drinks and then gets locked up for yelling at some stupid bartender who limits her drinks. She does not want this neurological current to play out.

STEP 3)   AUTOMATIC THINKING Lilian knows that she does not want the AUTOMATIC THINKING to be the BOSS OF HER BRAIN but it seems beyond her control. HE always makes her mad. It's HIS fault.

"How stupid can he be? He always does this," Lilian says to herself, as she recounts all the times he has messed up and gotten himself into situations that she ended up trying to fix.

STEP 4)   WEDGE - When the old current began to play out, Lilian considers her old way of reacting. It's a habit to yell, but it is not her only option. Her most useful WEDGE is walking away. Even though he is yelling at her as she walks out of the apartment, she keeps walking. It's the only way that she seems to be able to walk away from her AUTOMATIC THINKING and have time to get to her SMART THINKING.

Lilian is being the BOSS by not letting her AUTOMATIC THINKING become in charge. She knows she can create new thoughts, SMART THINKING.

Lilian put in her most successful WEDGE - she walked away. Now she needs to follow this new road, this alternate current of energy flowing through her body.

"I can't control what you do," she says to her boyfriend in a phone call from her apartment building, "and I am not trying to control you, but just remember your DUI. Remember that your insurance is expensive — you will get locked up, and the car will be impounded again if you are not careful and get pulled over. I don't think it is smart risking everything like that."

Whatever his response might be, Lilian begins to build a new neurological habit for herself without yelling. She got the AUTOMATIC THINKING to stop by placing a WEDGE, and she moved into SMART THINKING.

How her boyfriend processes her communication and how he responds is not the point. The only thing that matters is that Lilian begins to be the BOSS OF HER BRAIN and that she gets behind the steering wheel of her life. Lilian, and only Lilian, can break her yelling habit.

21 DAYS - It takes 21 days to make a new neurological habit. Lilian wants a new way of acting. She wants a new habit of responding. She remembers that only she can make her life better through her new habits. A new habit that she wants to have is being calmer, and handling things more powerfully.

She realizes after 21 days, it becomes almost automatic to respond in a calm manner. By slowing down before reacting, she yells less frequently, and she does not get sucked into anyone's drama.

After a while people begin to comment that she seems more calm. Their comments of support serve to reinforce her positive new habits. Lilian eventually finds that the power of changing her behavior through being the BOSS OF HER BRAIN is helpful in all areas of her life. She finds that she has developed a successful mastery of reactions; she has established new neurological rivers, which become a new neurological pathway in her body.

WHY IT WORKS

The human body is pretty simple to control when you understand how the body operates. You can decide to be the BOSS OF YOUR BRAIN.

What keeps us from changing bad habits? Fear. Fear of failure. Being too lazy to stick out the process of change. Low self-esteem. Not believing in yourself enough to know, deep down, that you can make your life powerfully good.

BOSS OF YOUR BRAIN provides the tools for you to be the boss, to get in the driver's seat, take control, and get rid of unproductive neurological pathways. You can completely control your actions and reactions when you fully master the concept of BOSS OF YOUR BRAIN.

Just a Thought

No matter what you know, or how smart you are -- you do not know all there is to know.

There will always be new, different and better ways to see things, and new information to experience. Because things are always changing, there is always a new way of being.

You are changing, even now, because as a human, you absorb information that your brain places into categories. You then assign a meaning to it, even if there is "no meaning." From that meaning you create your life. - Coach

BOSS OF YOUR BRAIN
In Action

SARA AND ANGER

Sara had a problem with her anger. Her father always yelled when he got angry, telling Sara that she was just like her mother. Her mother had a problem with anger, especially when she was drinking. Sara felt like she would never be able to change and that she was destined to be angry most of the time. Thoughts came into her mind that she could not control.

When she got angry, she often acted in ways that she regretted. She wished that she would not get so angry, but when her thoughts took over, she could not seem to stop them. Sara got irritated easily and blew up at the slightest provocation. People got on her nerves a lot.

Since her parents angered easily, Sara thought that she had no choice but to get angry as well. Sara felt out of control. She even got angry with herself for getting angry.

THINK ABOUT IT 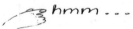 *hmm . . .*

How would Sara use the BOSS OF YOUR BRAIN tool to help with her anger? What actions will Sara need to put into practice to do; BOSS OF YOUR BRAIN?

STEP 1)   INFORMATION IN - Information comes into the very center of Sara's brain for processing through her sense of sight, smell, touch, hearing and taste. She begins her AUTOMATIC THINKING, using habits tucked in the back of her brain.

STEP 2)   ELECTRICAL CURRENT - Much like an electrical current, this information shoots through Sara's body with a meaning attached. She has created the meaning based on her prior experiences and expectations for the future. Because Sara is human, she naturally and automatically gives meaning to information that she experiences. Remember, Sara decides what things mean based on previous experiences and future expectations.

STEP 3) AUTOMATIC THINKING - When the old current of meaning begins to flow her AUTOMATIC THINKING begins to take over. Sara remembers the parts of the brain and she takes the control. She remembers BOSS OF YOUR BRAIN.

STEP 4) WEDGE – Sara knows that the only thing that can save her is if she gets her thoughts to be SMART THINKING rather than AUTOMATIC THINKING. For Sara, her WEDGE is calling a friend.

She pulls out her phone and starts to dial. Sometimes, just pulling out her phone is enough. Even leaving a message is helpful. She just needs a WEDGE to give her time to get her thinking into SMART THINKING.

Once Sara starts her SMART THINKING, she is starting to "re-wire" her physical neurology. She is actually building an alternate current of meaning. This alternate current of meaning is going to naturally modify Sara's reactions and actions.

21 DAYS - It takes about 21 days to replace an old habit and make a new neurological habit. Sara needs to remember...Sometimes, lasting change happens slowly. She just keeps moving forward.

OBSERVE OTHERS...

Spend a little time observing the bad habits that control the life experiences of the women around you. Neurological habits run the behavior of guards, staff, Bunkies, friends, family, employers and yourself. Everyone runs old, worn neurological habits.

Just observe and let the behaviors you see tell you about the habits of others. Let their habits tell you if they are the boss and in the driver's seat of their life, or if their brain is running on a tank full of negative habits.

Also, observe yourself...

Notice when you are the BOSS OF YOUR BRAIN. Can you begin to build new neurological habits? Which ones are habitual pathways that you would most benefit from re-wiring, or re-constructing?

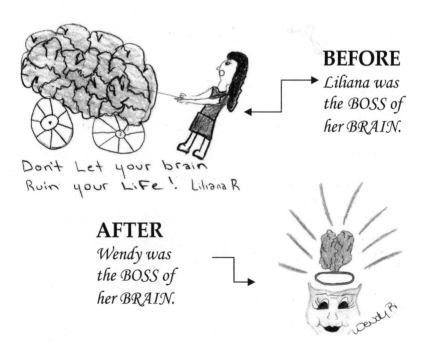

BEFORE
Liliana was the BOSS of her BRAIN.

Don't Let your brain Ruin your LiFe! Liliana R

AFTER
Wendy was the BOSS of her BRAIN.

BEFORE

Jamie was the BOSS of her BRAIN.

Art by Jamie W.

AFTER

Jamie was the BOSS of her BRAIN.

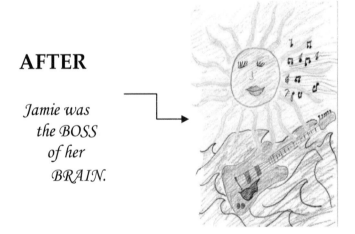

Words from GOGI Girl Laura W.

The one major thing that has been difficult for me to let go of in my life is my grandfather's death. When I was fifteen, I decided to move from my mom's in Virginia where I was raised, to my dad's in California, clear across the country.

I was raised by my mom. She was a single mom; I was a part-time latch-key kid and raised with the assistance of my grandparents. Since I only saw my real father on occasional weekends and summer vacations, my grandfather, Bop Bop, was the only real example of a man and a father in my life. I was the apple of Bop Bop's eye. His star, straight-A student, the first and only grandchild for quite awhile. I remember trips to the playground together, our daily after-dinner walks. Even trips to the drive-thru bank teller window to get that lollipop was an exciting and momentous occasion for me with my Bop Bop.

As I got older, so did Bop Bop. His lap began to feel uncomfortable underneath me. I'd sit on his rapidly growing gaunt lap in his big wing-backed chair with grease-stains from his hair in the corner of the living room listening to his narration of the Raggedy Ann & Andy book that I'd chosen for the day's reading. I became terrified of the stranger that began to drag the oxygen tank around with him everywhere he'd go as his emphysema worsened. Almost all of our special excursions became an impossibility for us. This is where I became terrified of losing my Bop Bop and began to alienate myself from the entire world.

My mom allowed me to follow through with my decision to move across the country on one condition, that I must tell Bop Bop myself. I knew how badly this would hurt him, because he loved me so much and was looking forward to seeing me graduate as one of the top ten dean's list honor students with a near perfect GPA.

Since I was moving to California to finish my last grade in high school, my mother made it apparent to me that Bop Bop wouldn't be able to fly 3,000 miles to see his "Little Mike" graduate.

Cont. next page

I was hoping my mom had forgotten that I hadn't confessed my plan to my grandparents yet and have to tell them herself after I was safely far away in sunny Southern Cali; however, that was not the case. My mom made a final pitstop before the airport...at my grandparents' house. Oh, no! I had to get brave and tell the truth.

I walked in. Quickly, I told Bop-Bop that I was moving to Dad's and not coming back. I gave him a hug and a kiss as I watched his heart break and he cried for the first time in my life. I couldn't bear the pain of hurting him so badly and I quickly turned and walked out the front door to never look back again...and to never see him alive again.

Bop Bop died about 6 months after I left Virginia. It's hard for me not to accept responsibility of his death. I feel that if I had stayed, he would've had something to live for and look forward to. I know he was terminally ill and getting worse every day, but I also know that one can will oneself to live.

Would he have lived longer and happier if I had stayed? Did he give up because he knew he would never see his Little Mike graduate and go on to be successful? Or, have I just used this experience to continuously self-destruct and destroy my life and the only success I may have obtained in my lifetime?

Time to stop making excuses and be accountable for my past decisions. Time to end the suffering I have brought into my life and to the lives of those who love me through my selfish choices I made in my addiction.

Laura W. - GOGI Campus President 2008

Art by Adrianne K.

CHAPTER 5

BELLY BREATHING

Words from Coach Taylor...

❧ *I believe it is physiologically impossible to be in rage and Belly Breathing at the same time. I also believe it is impossible to make bad decisions and Belly Breathe at the same time.*

❧ *If your first line of defense in taking back your life is to get in the habit of Belly Breathing, you are likely to Breathe your way into internal freedom. Belly Breathing is a powerful tool for you as you create new habits.*

Use this tool of Belly Breathing in the process of empowering yourself to make strong and solid decisions — to run your own life in a powerful manner. Remember to take your time and truly integrate the ideas into daily activities. The secret of making these tools work for you is to work on the tools. Practice them and integrate them into your daily life.

Practice the skill of BOSS OF YOUR BRAIN and you will begin to put the concepts into action automatically. Re-read and focus your efforts in the mastery of the first and most important component of your foundation—understanding and integrating the concepts of BOSS OF YOUR BRAIN.

This component is designed to help get you into the driver's seat, to give you control over your decisions and actions. You will be at the mercy of others until you realize that you can control your actions.

Take control of your life... ❖

BOSS OF YOUR BRAIN was designed as an easy way to empower you to take control of your life. Practice the BOSS OF YOUR BRAIN tool until you have a solid grasp on the power to re-direct and actually create new thoughts. Then, the other tools will help you reach your potential level of freedom.

You can think that you know all the tricks in the book, but if you do not know - deep down inside - that you are in charge of your own life, you are never completely free.

Part of what we do at GOGI is to teach potential volunteers the tools in this book. After they are taught the concept of BOSS OF YOUR BRAIN, they are given the tool of BELLY BREATHING. They are taught how to breathe only after they learn that they are the boss of their brain. Until they are in the driver's seat, it is not as powerful to have them breathing properly.

When you know that you are BOSS OF YOUR BRAIN and you breathe powerfully, you are able to consciously move oxygen throughout your body. When you consciously move oxygen throughout your body, your brain gets adequate oxygen for making positive decisions.

Don't let your brain betray you ❖

Your brain will only betray you when it is not under your control. When you forfeit your right to think and react in a manner that empowers you, it is because you have forgotten you are BOSS. The tools of BOSS OF YOUR BRAIN and BELLY BREATHING are designed to get you back in control. For many of you, it may be the first time you have been in control.

Many women are born into environments void of basic tools of self-empowerment and positive decision-making. Does this sound familiar? Perhaps your parents never taught you because they never learned the tools themselves.

Without information, how are you to learn? Self-empowerment is not taught in schools. It is often taught in sports or churches, but increasing numbers of women do not take advantage of these resources.

No more excuses

Now, however, you have no excuse. You can no longer blame your parents, society, or the system. You can no longer abdicate your right to create your own life and your personal internal freedom, because these tools are simple enough to use and fit into your daily life.

The GOGI tools are even taught to kindergarten children with great success. Of course, <u>you</u> can learn them. Of course, <u>you</u> can be successful. Just keep reading and re-reading. Keep practicing and practicing some more.

Art by JackiLyn S.

Successful students are the finest teachers. Your experiences with these concepts will enlighten and teach others.

It is <u>because</u> of your past that you have value and credibility to teach how to change your life. ☺

It is <u>because</u> of your record that you have value in helping women just like you.

Make the change <u>inside</u> you, then teach others what needs to be done!

Coach Taylor

Art by JackiLyn S.

I'm practicing my BELLY BREATHING.

Practice the concept of truly being in the driver's seat of your thoughts and behaviors. After you begin to grasp the power inherent in these concepts, think about sharing them. One way to really learn something is to talk about it and begin to teach what you have learned.

All the while, pay attention to your own ways of behaving. Really watch yourself operate and see where you do (and don't) have mastery. Once you have completed the mastery of BOSS OF YOUR BRAIN, then you move on to the concept of BELLY BREATHING.

Assuming that you have practiced BOSS OF YOUR BRAIN, let's move on to the next level of getting you in control of your life. You will learn about another powerful tool for improving your life. It is a very simple tool called:

☆   **"BELLY BREATHING"**   ☆

The most powerful tools that we have as women are often the most simple. You would think that breathing is natural, and that it is done correctly and automatically. However, this is not the case. You may also think that breathing properly is not very important. However, it is the most important thing that we can do for controlling our thoughts and automatic reactions.

When observing a baby's breathing, you will see his or her entire body expand and contract with every breath. You will see their little belly rise and fall as they effortlessly take in oxygen.

As you watch them, it seems as if their entire body fills with air because their little body expands and moves with every breath. It seems as if their entire body contracts and moves with every breath when the unused air is exhaled. This can be compared to a balloon as it moves and expands when it is filled with air.

Words from GOGI Girl Laura A.

Wow! Breathe. Breathe. Breathe. What an awesome tool to use when you're angry, scared or upset. While incarcerated, I have gotten angry on many occasions. When angry, I don't behave normally. And that made me make bad decisions. Going to lockup was the consequence.

Now that I have learned to breathe I learned to control my actions in a bad situation. The situation will not turn out worse. Breathe! Breathe! Breathe!

Take it from the little ones...

To breathe as effortlessly as a baby does is the natural process of breathing. If you observe adults, however, you will see a wide variety of breathing patterns. Most breathing patterns of adults are ineffectual at relieving stress. In some cases, breathing can provoke anxiety or rage.

You might notice that women who are stressed, chronically depressed, angry, or irritated have a breathing pattern that is very different from those who are relaxed and calm. The calm person's body moves and expands when they breathe. The uptight person's body is likely to remain rigid and stiff, as the air has a difficult time getting into the lungs.

A chronically angry person may attempt to become still and quiet. Yet, it is very likely that when she breathes, her chest will rise and fall rapidly. The shoulders of a stressed woman might noticeably rise and fall with every breath she takes.

Some women might appear to have no signs of breathing, as their body is so rigid and stressed that it barely moves. Stressed, angry or fearful women have fallen into the habit of breathing poorly. When a woman is breathing properly, the belly area will move in and out with every breath. In stressed women, sometimes the belly will not move at all.

FIGHT OR FLIGHT RESPONSE

Breathing automatically becomes rapid and localized in the chest area during states of anger, fear, danger, or heightened physiological awareness. Shallow breathing is a physiological response to the need to pump oxygen quickly into your lungs in response to immediate danger. This quick-fix response does not support the body's long-term success at relaxation.

When breathing rapidly, your body instantly enters a "Fight or Flight" response. The body is designed to react automatically to threats or impending danger. It is necessary for the logical part of the brain to shut down and let your animal instincts take over when threatened with the loss of life.

As the body enters a panicked state with shallow and rapid breathing, the "smart," or logical thinking shuts down. It automatically signals you to fight for your life or take flight and run to safety. This natural reaction is called the "Fight or Flight Response." Breathing so that air only gets into the chest is "shallow" breathing and is a natural defense mechanism designed to help you protect yourself when you need to act quickly to save your life.

Although it might help under threatening circumstances, this type of shallow or limited chest breathing can be disadvantageous in relationships. You are smarter, calmer, more powerful and able to make better decisions when you breathe in a relaxed manner. The angry, depressed, irritated individual usually utilizes chest breathing. Their entire body is missing out on much needed oxygen.

THE LIMBIC SYSTEM

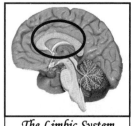

Let's look at an area inside the brain called the limbic system. The limbic system is a group of brain parts with many functions. One important job is to warn us when we are in situations of real or perceived danger.

The Limbic System is circled above.

When we believe that we are in danger, the limbic system sends out messages and our body reacts immediately. When we are anxious, angry, fearful, depressed or have similar emotions, it is likely that our limbic system is pumping cortisol and other chemicals into our blood system in amounts that alter our reactions.

High levels of cortisol can be counter productive

Cortisol is valuable as it gives us the ability to react to stressful situations in an immediate and urgent manner. Cortisol has an important function in your body. However, it is not useful when individuals experience or interpret an environment to be hostile. That is when it is delivered throughout the body constantly and continually.

Art by Davida M.

When too much cortisol pumps throughout your system, or other hormones and chemicals are out of balance, the signs become observable in the body. Women with tightly balled fists are usually operating from a stress-based, high cortisol-level way of being. Women with cold hands and feet, extra weight around their middle, and who breathe shallowly are likely to be suffering from high levels of stress and high levels of cortisol. It is interesting to note that when we get used to this type of functioning it becomes a neurological pathway and the body assumes it as a normal habit.

When we are stressed for a long period of time our body thinks, "Ok, this is how I am supposed to be. Stress is the natural state. Let me settle into pumping out more cortisol and tightening up my muscles." We might exist with high levels of cortisol and other "fight or flight" responses and think that it is normal. In some cases, we DO live in environments that are potentially dangerous and therefore our bodies are never given the opportunity to know what it is like to be physically at peace.

The truth of the matter

The truth of the matter is that the body was designed to breathe like a safe and healthy baby, with each and every part of the body gently expanding and contracting as we calmly inhale and exhale. BELLY BREATHING is a technique that works instantly on even the most habitual chest or shoulder breathing. This breathing technique is important for those having a difficult time controlling negative or unproductive thoughts or actions.

Scientific studies prove that breathing properly relaxes the mind and increases the likelihood that thoughts and actions can be controlled.

BELLY BREATHING will:

- Help Increase Positive Thoughts
- Decrease Sadness
- Decrease Loneliness
- Decrease Rage
- Decrease Depression
- Decrease Helplessness
- Decrease Grief
- Help Alleviate Addiction
- Increase Good Health
- Increase Optimism
- Increase Happiness

BELLY BREATHING is the legitimate shortcut to self-empowerment and enlightenment.

Coach Felicia poses with Inglewood City Chief of Police at an event honoring Inglewood's volunteers.

Coach Cathleen after a day volunteering with GOGI youth.

GOGI Coaches 2008

> *How many of you can begin to be a positive influence to other incarcerated individuals? How many of you will reach beyond the bars to your families and friends? What can you do today to share positive tools with others?*
>
> *Coach Taylor*

HOW DOES BELLY BREATHING WORK?

When you use **BELLY BREATHING**, oxygen flows into the lungs more effectively and your body is relaxed enough to process the oxygen optimally. Breathing this way allows your body to relax. Relaxed breathing allows you to make better decisions and handle adverse situations better.

ADDED BENEFITS OF BELLY BREATHING

There is an additional benefit to the **BELLY BREATHING** technique. When breathing with the stomach area, the muscles in that area become firmer and stronger. This is the kind of breathing that athletes use in their regular exercise regime to build strong, lean muscles in their stomach area.

Mastering **BELLY BREATHING** in every day life allows you to react differently to stress. An extra bonus is that you are likely to develop a firmer set of stomach muscles in the process.

Art by Taylor W.

Words from GOGI Girl Laura W.

The very first time I met Coach Taylor, she wrote in the first page of my GOGI book, "Laura, in the breath, you will find your freedom." Boy, was she right! My entire life, up to the point I retrained myself to belly breathe, had been led by poor choices and rash decision-making because I had been breathing shallowly with my chest.

As a result of my previously poor breathing habits, my life was a chaotic mess. Here I am back in jail after 14 years since my last trip and 8 years clean. What happened to my life? I now know that I never learned how to oxygenate my body. I learned at a very young age to breathe just like my mother, anxiously and shallowly through my chest.

My mom now goes to yoga to learn to breathe properly. With the help of Coach Taylor, I have now re-trained myself to belly breathe. I am armed with all these many self-empowering GOGI tools and ready to make good choices in my life, so I will be successful in my future.

HERE'S WHY BELLY BREATHING WORKS...

When you are angry, fearful, or in a state of rage, it is likely that you are breathing with limited oxygen into the lungs. It is likely that you breath with your chest rising and falling. Your belly is likely to remain still. "Chest breathing" limits the amount of oxygen available throughout your body.

Can you tell if you are BELLY BREATHING or chest breathing as you read? Reading is usually a relaxing activity and it could be that your belly expands and contract during this relaxed state.

How are you breathing right this very moment? Is your belly rising and falling with each breath? When there is limited oxygen in the body, you cannot fully function. With limited oxygen, "smart" decisions get put to the side and "emergency" or "panic" decisions move into panic actions. Panic decisions and panic actions are rarely to your advantage.

HOW TO DO <u>BELLY BREATHING</u>

If you can control your thoughts, you can control your actions. And you can control the way you respond to the actions of others. An action is always preceded by a thought, even when we are not aware of the thought. A major tool in controlling your thoughts is simply getting oxygen to the entire brain and throughout your entire body.

As simple as it seems, BELLY BREATHING and the act of getting the proper amount of oxygen to the entire body is likely to change your actions when you are angry or upset.

Here are the three simple steps for BELLY BREATHING.

STEP 1) SOLID GROUND - No matter what is going on, think about how firmly your feet are on the ground. Think about placing them firmly on the earth as you begin the process of BELLY BREATHING. Plant your feet on solid ground. People are usually better breathers if they feel solid.

STEP 2) FILL YOUR FEET - One way that helps women who are really stuck in bad breathing patterns is to have them pretend and use their imagination. If you are having a difficult time getting effortless breath into your lungs so that your body will process that oxygen optimally, here is a little trick that works wonders on the most difficult or tense women.

Imagine for a moment that you need to fill your feet up with air. Imagine that your lungs, which are in your chest area, are actually in your feet. It might seem funny to pretend that your lungs are actually located in your feet; but, this technique works wonders at getting the body prepared for optimal breathing.

Imagine that your feet expand and contract like two balloons filling up with air each time you breathe. This trick works perfectly to help the body do what it is designed to do and get fresh oxygen into the entire blood stream.

STEP 3) BELLY BREATHE - Fill your stomach area like filling a balloon as you inhale. When you inhale, imagine that there is a balloon in your belly and as you take in air the balloon expands. The more you inhale air the bigger the belly-balloon gets.

When exhaling, pull your belly button to your spine. If you are not certain you are doing it properly, try this trick before you fall asleep. Lay on your back. Place a book or your hand over your belly button. Just observe.

Do nothing but feel what happens as the air moves in and out of your body. Take some time and just watch your belly area. As you inhale, notice that when air comes into your body, your lungs fill up and your belly fills up. Likewise, when air leaves your body, watch as your body and hand on your belly moves lower toward your spine.

Do it this night after night. You will become aware of a new breathing pattern that will soon extend into the daylight hours. BELLY BREATHING will help you master relaxed breathing.

THINK ABOUT IT

Sometimes women get so angry that they make bad decisions or act in ways that they would not normally behave. When your body is running its own program and automatically reacting from high levels of cortisol, it may seem impossible to STOP the anger or the unproductive thought or feeling.

Do you remember a time when you were so angry or afraid that it seemed as if your body just took over? Most of us have "lost control" of our actions or reactions at one time or another.

When you lost control, did you react in a way that was unproductive or harmful to yourself or others? Take a moment to observe how you are breathing right at this moment.

Art by Davida M.

Words from GOGI Girl Zel O.

Belly breathing allows my entire body to become more relaxed. A relaxed body is inclined to make positive and powerful decisions.

Does your chest move when you breathe? Does your stomach move up and down when you breathe? Does your chest and stomach move at the same time? Do your shoulders move? Do you have control over your breathing? Can you selectively move your chest or your stomach when you breathe?

Go easy on yourself

Go easy on yourself when learning this and all self-empowerment techniques. Remember, sometimes lasting change happens slowly and over time. You may also be working to get rid of "bad" habits that you've had for a long time.

Lastly, give change an honest chance and keep practicing. Eventually, your body will create the new habit that will serve to your advantage. You may not even notice the changes. That does not matter. Just keep moving forward. It takes about 21 days to create a new neurological habit inside your body. Keep practicing week after week and before you know it, you will have created a new neurological habit for yourself.

Remember that somewhere very early in your childhood you developed habits due to your experiences and environment. You might have heard gunshots on a playground that frightened you. Like the 5th grader in Watts, California, you may have developed a physiological coping tool that caused you to breathe from a state of fear.

The good news is the fact that you can change how your body responds to almost anything. Continue to practice BOSS OF YOUR BRAIN and BELLY BREATHING. They work to assist you in the changes that will undoubtedly improve your life.

WATCH OTHERS

Observation of others gives you vital information and places you in a powerful position of knowledge. Just observe people when they get angry. Watch how they are breathing. You might notice that most people's breathing gets short and shallow when they are in a state of anger or rage. Fists might ball up, faces get red, and actions become abrupt or forceful. When people breathe this way, they are not relaxed and they are not making the smartest decisions.

You will know if someone is breathing poorly if his or her chest rises and falls with each breath. If a person is doing BELLY BREATHING, their chest will remain still and the stomach area will go in and out with every breath.

BELLY BREATHING is an easy tool for you to use when you need to take complete control of your body. BELLY BREATHING helps to relax your body to allow you access to better decision making skills.

MEGANC.

Do you like the outcome of using drugs? Remember the pain and hurt that using drugs caused you and others.

Change your bad habits into good ones.

BELLY BREATHING
In Action

JENNY QUITS SMOKING WEED

Jenny, 27, has smoked weed with her brothers since she was 9 years old. All her troubles still seem to go away for a while when she is loaded.

She has been clean for two weeks now, but she is more irritable and angry than usual. Jenny and her partner broke up a few days ago and she is thinking that she should call to see if they can work it out. She goes over to her friend's house to think about things. She is greeted by several people that she knows and they are partying and having a good time.

As if that wasn't enough to make her start smoking again, the worst part of it is the fact that her partner is sitting on the couch just a bit too close to one of her best friends. Her thoughts run wild and she wants to strike out at her partner and her friend.

To let BELLY BREATHING work for her, Jenny needs to take control. She remembers that she knows how to do BELLY BREATHING, which is her tool to use any time she wants to take control of a situation and do things differently.

She remembers the steps to BELLY BREATHING. No matter how mad she is at her partner, she knows she is the BOSS OF HER BRAIN and that her life is up to her. She puts BELLY BREATHING into action.

Art by Laura A.

BELLY BREATHING IN ACTION

1) SOLID GROUND - Jenny feels her feet firmly on the ground. She lets herself feel more solid with both feet firmly on the ground. She can be very firm about what is good for her and what she wants to do when she feels solid. Jenny is committed to herself to quit smoking weed—she is solid and wants to be strong.

2) FILL THE FEET - Jenny imagines what it would be like if her lungs are in her feet and she breathes as if she must fill up her feet with air. This is an easy way to get oxygen throughout her body. Her body relaxes a little. She can remember what she wants with her life. She is the boss and in control of her thoughts and actions.

She feels solid and strong when she gets breath all the way to her feet. Breathing this way permits her to be firm about her commitment to quit smoking weed.

3) BELLY BREATHE - Jenny turns her focus to her stomach area. She takes a deep breath and lets her stomach expand like a balloon filling up with air. When she exhales, she pulls her belly button tightly inward toward her spine.

When Jenny breathes this way, it allows her entire body to relax. She has a better focus on her goals and does not let anyone or anything pull her off track when her body relaxes.

Belly Breathing
Try It, Close your eyes. Fill up your feet with air. Now, feel the air going in and out of your body,

WHY IT WORKS

BELLY BREATHING helps move oxygen throughout Jenny's body. When Jenny gets air throughout her body, it places her in a more relaxed state. Jenny can think smartly when she is relaxed and she remembers that she has control over her thoughts and actions.

She makes better decisions when she is relaxed. She can now think BEYOND the immediate situation and into the future with BELLY BREATHING.

She can avoid thoughts and actions that would take her away from what she really wants. She is learning that she can focus on positive outcomes that will bring peace of mind.

OBSERVE OTHERS...

Observe others and their breathing patterns. Notice guards who have shallow breathing. Pay attention to women coming out of chapel or yoga class. Do they breathe differently? Who is uptight and who is relaxed? How do their breathing patterns betray their truth?

In a short amount of time, just by observing someone's breathing patterns, you may begin to predict if they are going to "lose it" or if they are dealing resourcefully in a situation.

Also, observe yourself...

Notice when you are BELLY BREATHING. Does your stomach rise and fall with every breath? Can you move the breathing from your chest to your stomach and back again? Take notice of who is in charge of your body's breathing if and when you lose control.

TOOLS FOR THE MIND

"Looking Into The Future."
-Sharity A.

Getting Out
GO
By Going In

Art by Taylor W.

GOGI Girl Coco, is pictured with
GOGI Coach, Andrea, at the GOGI
Campus offices in Lynwood, California.

GOGI Girl Aura with her two sons.

GOGI Girl Coco, is pictured with her son,
Jakari. Coco and Jakari volunteer
at the GOGI offices, helping to process
homework, internet research and
support for reentry students.
Coco was one of the first students
at GOGI Campus. She has recently
enrolled in psychology courses

GOGI Girl Jillian
has enrolled in
college to be a
drug treatment
counselor.

CHAPTER 6

FIVE SECOND LIGHTSWITCH

"In just 5 seconds I can change my thoughts."
- by Jennifer B

The process of internal freedom comes in the steps taken toward your self-empowerment. They are similar to building a house. You cannot paint the walls before laying the foundation.

The first two tools: BOSS OF YOUR BRAIN and BELLY BREATHING lay the foundation for lasting and profound change.

Make certain you have a firm grasp of the concepts presented and that you are able to use them fairly effortlessly. It is absolutely fine, normal and expected if it takes you longer than one week to completely "get" a concept.

Some GOGI students take up to a month to grasp the idea that they are the boss, and that their brain is under control. Others take weeks and weeks to relearn how to breathe properly.

While some people say they understand a concept, they may still blame everyone else for their situation. This is not a firm foundation from which to empower your life. This is not freedom. It is actually abdicating power by handing the driving wheel over to the person who made you upset.

By taking total responsibility for your life, these tools will become powerfully effective.

When you are ready, and feel as if BOSS OF YOUR BRAIN and BELLY BREATHING are easy, add FIVE SECOND LIGHTSWITCH.

FIVE SECOND LIGHTSWITCH may challenge everything you've learned about breaking bad habits. It is likely you have been told, "Don't think about it," or "Put it out of your mind," when you're confronted with the temptation to return to an old, worn and undesirable behavior.

It is not easy for women to walk away from old habits, or ways of behaving or thinking. It takes a rare woman to walk away from a bad habit without a struggle – I offer congratulations to those who can.

Many people, however, need to gradually incorporate new habits and realities when processing change. The FIVE SECOND LIGHTSWITCH is an easy tool for breaking bad habits because it acknowledges that all thoughts are powerful.

The **FIVE SECOND LIGHTSWITCH** will help you:
- Take control of thoughts that are bad habits.
- Take control of feelings that you cannot "get away" from your bad habit.
- Take control of actions that result from your thoughts and feelings.

FIVE SECOND LIGHTSWITCH
*will allow you to work WITH your mind
instead of against it.*
FIVE SECOND LIGHTSWITCH
*will allow you to experience your
ability to control your actions.*
FIVE SECOND LIGHTSWITCH
*will permit distance from disabling habits and
empower you to change other behaviors as well.*

*Coach Taylor receives
acknowledgement from the
CGA Men at CMC.*

*Words from GOGI Girl
Lilian R.*

Gogi
Entitled
To
Teach
Individuals
New
Goals

Outstanding
Unbelievable
Tools

Beyond
Your

Greatest
Obstacles
In
New
Gracious

Incredible N'
Numerous ways

Words from a GOGI Girl

Drugs will...
Take you farther than you want to go
Cost you more than you want to spend
Keep you longer than you want to stay

--Unknown Author, Submitted by Laura W.

HOW DOES THE LIGHTSWITCH WORK?

When you try to stop thinking about your temper, it seems that all you can think about is your temper. When you try to stop thinking about your soon-to-be ex or your divorce, it seems that all you can think about is your soon-to-be ex or your divorce. When you are trying to lose weight and you tell yourself not to think about food, it seems that all you can think about is food.

Most of the time, telling yourself to stop a thought just isn't going to work. Sometimes, in fact, it has an opposite effect.

FIVE SECOND LIGHTSWITCH is effective as it works on the belief that thoughts are like rivers of information flowing through the body. You can frantically build a dam to stop a river's flow. Or, you can gently divert the water and let it run in another direction.

FIVE SECOND LIGHTSWITCH gently re-directs the water towards a better, more productive flow.

HERE'S WHY THE LIGHTSWITCH WORKS...

FIVE SECOND LIGHTSWITCH works because most people have a difficult time "stopping," or often have an easier experience "replacing." The Five Second Lightswitch is a "wedge" placed in the current flow of neurons that sends information down another, more productive path.

Ask a child to stop a behavior and it is likely that they will continue. Their focus is on the undesirable behavior — they don't know what to do as a replacement for it, or how to promote positive actions. When you divert a child's attention by offering an alternative, you are stopping the undesirable behavior.

In the following example the mother gave Monica something to move toward, something more productive to do with her energy and focus. Giving yourself something else to do with your thoughts is why FIVE SECOND LIGHTSWITCH works.

Words from GOGI Girl Wendy R.
This tool really works. I love it. Often
when I'm about to get mad,
I stop and think...is this going to matter
five years from now?
Then I start to laugh within
my head, and walk away.
Thank you Coach Taylor for
my new tool for life, the
Five Second Lightswitch.

Monica and the Hot Pan

"Monica, don't touch the pan. It's hot," the mom blurts out to her 3 year-old daughter who is reaching up to the pan handle sticking out from the stove just above her head.

Monica hears the warning but her focus is on grabbing the pan handle. More attention is given to the pan by hearing its name — so even when she says "don't," her mind is still focused on the pan.

Monica then has to include both what her mom said about the pan and the word "don't" in her analysis of the communication. Sometimes we focus on one portion of the communication but fail to remember the "don't" part.

Monica's hand reaches up for the pan.

"Monica, I told you, don't touch that pan," her mom yells louder. "You bad girl. You never listen to me."

Poor Monica is left standing there crying and confused, with a pan full of food splattered all over mom's clean floor.

Monica and the Hot Pan – The Remix

Monica toddles over to the pan area. Seeing pending danger, the mom gently diverts her attention.

"Monica? Hey, look at this," her mom says, holding her fork up in the air with her mashed potatoes balanced expertly.

"Can you help me put these potatoes in my mouth?"

Monica automatically toddles over to where her mother has placed her focus. She helps mom put the fork in her mouth, she feels an increase in personal value and self-esteem and mom doesn't need to mop the floor.

"You are so smart, Monica," the mom says.

Now she can personally take her to the stove and explain why she moves the handle from her reach.

"This is very hot. It hurts to touch things that are hot," she tells her.

HOW THE LIGHTSWITCH WORKS

Instead of attempting to immediately STOP the river of thoughts leading to undesirable behavior, let's see if THE FIVE SECOND LIGHTSWITCH is an easier way for you to take control of your life.

THE FIVE SECOND LIGHTSWITCH

STEP 1) THOUGHTS ENTER - A thought enters your mind. "I really wish I could have just one cigarette right now. I really need it, I am so stressed." Or, "I will go back for seconds of this meal; it is actually pretty good, for once." Or, "She makes me so mad. The only times that she listens is when I get angry."

STEP 2) PERMISSION GRANTED - Instead of being upset that you are reverting back to old thoughts, permit those thoughts to toss around in your head for a few seconds. There was a time when those old thoughts served you well by making you feel temporarily better, more powerful, safer, stronger....whatever...

You need to permit the THOUGHT (not the action) to exist for FIVE SECONDS. Ask yourself, "It served me once but no longer serves me to think this way. Why am I thinking that particular thought?" In those five seconds, think about how the old behavior worked for you. "Cigarettes calmed me down when nothing else would." Or, "If I don't eat now, who knows when I will get something that tastes good." Or, "When I got angry it seemed like she listened more."

1 - 2 - 3 - 4 - 5
LIGHTSWITCH !

STEP 3) THOUGHT SWAP - For five seconds you have considered all the old benefits of the old behavior. When you get to the sixth second, swap the thought to something, anything leading you away from the old behavior.

It's like turning on a light switch and heading the neurons in a more productive direction – a direction that is completely under your control.

"Cigarettes calm me, however: 1) they are expensive, 2) they may shorten my life, and 3) I will be healthier, smell better and be stronger by not smoking."

STEP 4) REPEAT REPEAT REPEAT - If the bad habit thought comes back after the sixth second you will repeat, repeat, repeat the process of FIVE SECOND LIGHTSWITCH, reminding yourself of the new direction you are taking with your thoughts and actions.

Eventually, the thought about the bad habit will be overruled by the unrelenting persistence of the new thought. If you keep this up long enough, FIVE SECOND LIGHTSWITCH will become automatic and, eventually, you will have a new way of thinking.

Your biggest challenge might be to maintain the change. In the equation for change explained earlier in this book, DATA (information) needs to be combined with SPACE (time and room for change) and then a SHIFT occurs. This results in changes.

The part of the process that may get discouraging is when the external environment or our own internal environment does not provide enough SPACE for the change to hold.

HOW NEURONS WORK

We learned with BOSS OF YOUR BRAIN that neurons are message holders and neurotransmitters are the delivery service of the messages. Neurons need to transport a new message to change a bad habit. The neurotransmitter need to be told to take new messages to a new and different place resulting in new and different emotions and actions. FIVE SECOND LIGHTSWITCH helps you accomplish this task.

The key to FIVE SECOND LIGHTSWITCH is that you must repeat and repeat and repeat the process until the new neurological pathways are secured.

New thoughts are like a wedge, leading thoughts in a different direction toward success. Keep putting wedge after wedge in and eventually the neurological river will get the idea that you are no longer feeding the bad habit. It WILL automatically follow your new directions – in about 21 days.

Freeway traffic is easily diverted

It is easier to re-direct traffic on a freeway than to stop traffic altogether. The neurology of your body is similar to traffic on a freeway. If you want cars to travel down a different road, you are going to have to put up a roadblock to move the traffic in the desired direction.

You need to be persistent in swapping the thought. Eventually, the traffic will get the idea that the old freeway is not going to be traveled. When you break an old habit, you actually create an alternate neurological pathway, or "freeway" of communication inside your body.

Permitting the old thought to exist for five full seconds, and then consciously replacing it with another thought, is like diverting traffic instead of trying to stop it head on. Stopping an entire freeway of traffic is not easy, but getting drivers to take a new off-ramp is more effective, because it is less stressful, demanding, causes fewer collisions and promotes a smoother transition.

THINK ABOUT IT

What habits have you attempted to stop "cold turkey?" If you didn't quite accomplish your goal, ask yourself if the FIVE SECOND LIGHTSWITCH would have been a better option for you. When you take the opportunity to really consider your thought process, you are actually creating opportunities for change.

The more you consider alternatives in behavior the more likely that you will be to begin to test them out. Remember, everyone has automatic actions and reactions that they would like to change.

Oftentimes, it seems difficult to change these habits. We accept having a temper, eating improperly, being lazy, getting jealous, or stealing as just the way that we are "wired." We begin to accept that the undesirable behavior is unmanageable or "just who we are."

The FIVE SECOND LIGHTSWITCH is another powerful tool for you to use when beginning to reconstruct your internal wiring.

You now have BOSS OF YOUR BRAIN, BELLY BREATHING and the FIVE SECOND LIGHTSWITCH to help you in the process of creating new and positive neurological pathways.

Go easy on yourself in this process of taking control of your life and implementing lasting change. You have undoubtedly been responding and reacting in ways that have been familiar for quite some time. It will take a while to get just as familiar with new ways of thinking and being. Don't give up.

Change sometimes takes a while

Remember that, sometimes, lasting change happens slowly and may take a long time — especially when we break or change old habits by replacing them with new ways of thinking, behaving or believing.

Sometimes, change is so slow that we don't even know it is happening. Trust the process and just keep moving forward. Usually, those who are consistent with slow and steady changes are more successful at maintaining those changes over time. They keep moving forward even if they mess up, and are likely to be happier and more successful in the long haul.

When an individual constantly moves toward new ways of thinking and being, it is likely the changes will last for a long time.

- How would the FIVE SECOND LIGHTSWITCH work for you?

- What would be the automatic thoughts you would want to change?

- How would your life be different?

Art by Davida M.

One step at a time

Changing one habit, one way of thinking at a time will permit you to master your changes in small doses. Focus on wiring one room at a time, instead of trying to re-wire an entire house all at once.

Women often become over-enthusiastic. They set high expectations and suddenly become overwhelmed. They get irritated and blame an ineffective process for their failure. Some people claim that they are different and have tried everything. Or, they simply "cannot change." Perhaps they did not want to change in the first place.

The process of change is actually predictable. When DATA or information is available, the process of change begins. When there is enough SPACE for the information to grow into new ideas and new thoughts, then the process of change continues with a SHIFT. When CHANGE happens and it is sustained for a long enough period to form a habit within the body, the process of change has completed its' cycle.

Everyone can change how they think, how they act, how they react and how they feel. The SPACE + DATA + SHIFT = CHANGE equation describes the process.

Gather your information (DATA). Give yourself room inside your head and with your actions for it to have a positive effect (SPACE). You will eventually SHIFT and get the CHANGE you long to experience. Sustain that CHANGE long enough and you will have new, automatic habits.

Remember...

SPACE + DATA + SHIFT = CHANGE

OBSERVE

Observation of others will give you vital information and place you in a powerful position of knowledge. It will also let you see what is and what is not working for them. Ask others how they broke a bad habit. If they gave it up "cold turkey," what did they do in place of the bad habit? Could it be that they used their own version of FIVE SECOND LIGHTSWITCH when they gave up their habit?

Words from GOGI Girls Jennifer B. & Kimberly L.

THINGS I NEED TO LET GO OF....
~ My recent tragedy. ~ My bad habits of drug & alcohol abuse. ~ My worries. ~ My past. ~ My love and concern for certain people. ~ The people I have been around.   -Jennifer B.

LET GO
~ Evil thoughts.~ Fear of man.~ Drugs & alcohol.~ People, places & things (Old).~ Trying to keep up with the Jones'.~ Bad relationship.~ My past.~ Of being a bad mother, sister & friend.   -Kimberly L.

Davida M.

CONSIDER THIS...

FIVE SECOND LIGHTSWITCH
is a powerful tool for diverting the neurological
traffic reinforcing a bad habit.

FIVE SECOND LIGHTSWITCH
will empower you to consider the reasons you
decided to give up the habit in the first place.

FIVE SECOND LIGHTSWITCH
will allow you to create NEW thoughts,
new behaviors and new habits.

Words from GOGI Girl Doris S.

My Thoughts

I think some women are just not ready to quit. You might need to be at a point when you are really tired of the way things are going.

Stop and take a minute to think. The change you need to do is for you. Just in case that doesn't work, then it is OK to do it for someone else. The point is to do it.

I also think many women won't change because they don't have enough support from their family because they eventually stop believing in family. They failed many times before because they don't have anyone to encourage them.

But we are all still worth it. It would help at least to listen to others and show that we are not alone.

FIVE SECOND LIGHTSWITCH
In Action

THE GUARD

Let's say there is one particular guard who really has it out for you. We will call her C.O. Difficult. C.O. Difficult never liked you and you are not quite certain what you may have done to get her so focused on making your life miserable.

C.O. Difficult is having a particularly bad day. It seems that everyone in the yard is suffering from a severe case of raw nerves. Spirits are low. The newly arrived warden seems to be wielding his authority in some interesting ways, undoubtedly rattling C.O. Difficult and the other guards with new task lists and requirements.

It is movement time for your area and you are headed to work in the kitchen. C.O. Difficult yells across the yard for you to come over to her. You are irritated because you can't be late for work. You hope C.O. Difficult isn't going to pull anything stupid because you are just about ready to tell her where she can shove it. When she tells you to go to "A" Unit to deliver a message you respond, "What's your radio for?"

Instantly you know there's more in store from C.O. Difficult and you regret mouthing off. FIVE SECOND LIGHTSWITCH empowers you to handle C.O. Difficult and people like C.O. Difficult more effectively. Your <u>reaction</u> to "C.O. Difficults" of the world speaks everything about who you are.

The world knows about people like C.O. Difficult. They see this type of person moving through life in their self-consumed, miserable manner. What they do not know is how you react to the "C.O. Difficults" of the world. How you react says everything about you and nothing about C.O. Difficult.

FIVE SECOND LIGHTSWITCH IN ACTION

1) THOUGHTS ENTER - The desire to haul off and plant a firm fist into C.O. Difficult's blabbering mouth is pretty strong. She has pushed you beyond an acceptable limit and you have just got to set this guard straight.

2) PERMISSION GRANTED - Instead of being upset that you are having these thoughts, you let your mind notice this urge. In fact, think about what is happening with your thoughts for a full five seconds. You can even entertain the outcome if you were to act on your urge.

Let the THOUGHT (not the action) exist for FIVE FULL SECONDS. There was a time when acting on these kinds of thoughts was something you just automatically did without thinking. Notice that, too.

For five full seconds you can just think about what you are thinking about. Isn't it interesting how automatic your reaction to C.O. Difficult became? It is almost as if C.O. Difficult knew which buttons to push. She pushed them and you reacted like a puppet.

3) THOUGHT SWAP – Now, you will swap the thought for something more powerful. On the sixth second, you take over the wheel of the car and head in a different direction.

What it is going to take to get back on the job and away from a heated situation? Think to yourself, "I want peace more than I want to spend a week in the hole. What can I do to make peace right now?" Or, perhaps, "This is an old pattern that never worked for me. No matter if I'm right or wrong, it is time to do things differently."

4) REPEAT REPEAT REPEAT - You can think and re-think new ways of responding while C.O. Difficult's temperature begins to boil.

Take a subtle step back to get a bit more physical distance between you and C.O. Difficult. Take a deep breath using BELLY BREATHING and take control of the wheel of the car and do what you need to do to steer yourself to safety.

In this case, your RESULTS are more important than what you believe is RIGHT. Nothing that you say is going to change the fact that C.O. Difficult thinks she is right. There is no room for discussion. C.O. Difficult may write you up for being disrespectful and not following an order. She will be correct and you will spend some dark days thinking about how much you hate her, how right you were, and how you can't wait to see her on the street one day.

Instead, flip a light switch in your mind. Realize old ways of behaving are no longer out of your control. You have the power to send the neurological river anywhere that <u>you</u> choose to send it. As corny as it sounds on paper, you may choose to say to C.O. Difficult, "It was out of line for me to say that. I didn't mean to pop off. For some reason things seem tense on the yard for me today." Or you can stand neutral and say nothing, choosing to wait for a repeat of the order that will help you decide the quickest plan to get back to work.

WHY IT WORKS

FIVE SECOND LIGHTSWITCH works and becomes easier over time. FIVE SECOND LIGHTSWITCH allows you to "go with the flow" and also change its direction. It is easier to move traffic to the left or right than to stop a line of fast moving cars head on. Your automatic responses are like rivers of information flowing through your body.

Don't spend a large amount of time thinking about them when you can take action to divert the flow of information and achieve more positive reactions. Think of it like a river. It's easier to divert water running down a river than it is to stop the river's flow altogether.

FIVE SECOND LIGHTSWITCH works because it puts you in the position of acknowledging a bad habit or automatic thought and then moving beyond it. It diverts your attention toward the desired response. In this way, you acknowledge that the water is  flowing and you subtly divert it to a new direction. It is easier to divert running water than stop it. If a car is going in the wrong direction, rather than jerk the wheel to steer it, try gently guiding it back to where you want it to go.

You can let the moods, words, actions and reactions of others pull you off course. Or, you can make the decision to nudge yourself back on course by using the tools that you have gathered thus far: BOSS OF YOUR BRAIN, BELLY BREATHING, FIVE SECOND LIGHTSWITCH. Pull these tools out of your toolbox whenever they are needed.

It is inevitable that you will change. You will continue to change throughout your life. As you widen your perspective, you will begin to notice how others operate and why they operate in the manner that they do. Through your awareness, you will start to notice how you can stealthily avoid ninety-nine percent of confrontations and obstacles.

Begin to observe others around you. Through observation, you will learn from the mistakes and accomplishments of others.

OBSERVE OTHERS...

Take a few moments today to speak less. Observing the habits of others is usually easier if you keep your own thoughts silent. You can begin to witness their automatic reactions and automatic behaviors. You might observe them abdicating their ability to create the kind of life that they want. Then, you will see how powerless they truly have become. You will see that, for all their posturing and tough guy talk, they are really at the mercy of situations and others around them.

How would you use THE FIVE SECOND LIGHTSWITCH if you were suffering from old patterns of behavior of others that continue day after day? What new habit would you create as a replacement?

Also, observe yourself...

When could you begin to use the FIVE SECOND LIGHTSWITCH as a tool to get you back in the driver's seat of your life? Try the FIVE SECOND LIGHTSWITCH in one specific area of your life. Test it out long enough to let it work. Maybe you can pick one person and begin to build an alternate response pattern to their predictable communication. By the way, the FIVE SECOND LIGHTSWITCH helps enormously with two of the most powerful automatic habits to which people give up their power — drug addiction and compulsive thoughts.

Art by
Davida
M.

Words from GOGI Girl Bridgette

Everybody wants their freedom. Everybody wants that special someone to love, but everybody should wanna change. I've been here and there, but nowhere like here, where you're surrounded by white walls.

GOGI Girl Bridgette & son Elijah.

The tears that never stop falling from the eyes, the screams, moans and cries you hear through the night from different cells. My feelings started to take over me completely. I felt like the white walls were caving in on me. My own thoughts, memories and emotions were taking me away.

I started to look up to God, asking "Is this the end of me?!" I prayed throughout all of my days, asking God to forgive me and to help me. I kept my faith and drowned in the word of God. I asked God for a program or something to do with my time, I asked every day, until one day a talent show came, "GOGI" was their name, the show was wonderful and amazing. It inspired me so much.

I am a GOGI Girl as of today, and I'm happy. Yeah, I came a long way, but I'm thankful I'm here today. Yes, I miss my family true enough. I do get homesick constantly, but like Coach says,

"Bridgette, you gotta toughen up, be strong! Don't give up! Be the Boss of your Brain, use the Five Second Lightswitch, do your Positive What If's and your Positive TWA's. Step up!"

I love Coach Taylor. This GOGI program is teaching me a lot. I'm very much thankful and grateful for being here in the GOGI program. Thank you, Coach Taylor.

I still wanna go home! I'm looking on the bright side (Mom & Dad, I'll be home soon) ♥ I love you.♥

CHAPTER 7

WHAT IF?

Your intention becomes your reality

By now, you might be seeing small and subtle differences in your life if you are reading this book with the sincere intent of creating a powerful life for yourself.

Your experiences with others might be different. It might be clearer to see new opportunities or obstacles. You might be irritated that people around you are not in control of their thinking or

"What If I changed my friends."
By Jennifer B.

behaving. If things are subtly changing, either negatively or positively, then you are benefiting from:

The SPACE + DATA + SHIFT = CHANGE equation

- SPACE is room in your thinking that helps you consider options for your life. . .
- You may be benefiting from new DATA or new information, and you are giving yourself. . .
- A SHIFT of perception, and you are primed for
- CHANGE, as new behaviors and reactions begin to occur.

Art by Davida M.

Know your tools. Practice the tools you have learned so far until they become second nature. Your tools are:

1) BOSS OF YOUR BRAIN

2) BELLY BREATHING and

3) FIVE SECOND LIGHTSWITCH

Along the path of your journey, you may have modified or altered some of the steps to fit your own unique interpretation or style. Great. Make them yours. Put your unique stamp on the way you run your personal thought process.

The tools are not designed to fit every individual in the same way. They are flexible generalities that can be adjusted to fit your own interpretation or success strategies.

If these tools work exactly as described…that's great. It's also fine if they need a little modification to fit your own personal needs. The point is that you may fine-tune the tools and make them yours.

These tools permit new DATA (new information delivered in a new way), and allow you the SPACE (the internal environment), to "re-wire" your brain for the SHIFT leading to CHANGE.

As you begin to put these tools into practice, you will likely realize that you can control these tools in addition to controlling your thoughts.

The WHAT IF? tool for your toolbox of change is more concept related. Rather than a tangible or physiological process, WHAT IF? will tap into your unlimited potential for imagination and creativity.

This tool gives you permission to imagine possibilities, consider options, and provide a direction of which you can steer your intentions.

Words from GOGI Girl Felicia (Mimi) J.

This GOGI chapter lets you look at incarceration to use it as a tool for change. Having been incarcerated on and off for more than twenty years I can say that inside is not a place or space for easily renewing the mind or rehabilitating and stepping into my greatness.

On the contrary, the environment and the system are not set up that way. But, if you are willing while being incarcerated you can really look inside yourself. You will see how you have been rescued by coming to jail or prison.

The WHAT IF that Coach Taylor speaks about is the vision of what she sees inside the women doing time. I have the same vision for you and for myself. Internally, my WHAT IF is that I can help others achieve what I see so clearly in them. Helping the lifers in prison. Clearly a big WHAT IF.

I continue to work toward my dream of having a go-between prison and community for lifers. Getting them back to life. Giving lifers re-born hope of gaining back their life.

Perception is the key. Action makes the WHAT IF powerful. Seeing past my self-imposed limitation is will, growth, desire.... Action is the key to WHAT IF.

The next tool is WHAT IF?

In truth, no one has control over your thoughts. No person, no event, no situation, no punishment, no mistake, no phone call or judge's gavel has control over your thoughts. And, no person, no event, no situation, no punishment, no mistake, no phone call or judge's gavel has control over your reactions to anything in your life.

There are unlimited ways to experience each event. Here is an example of how people perceive their surroundings differently:

What if our society was truly under siege and the only safe place was inside a State or Federal prison? Would your experience behind the wall be different?

Art by Deanna H.

What If these shapes became a larger picture? Make it happen!

Words from GOGI Girl Stacy P.

I believe I can help future GOGI students by letting them know how the bad choices I made...put me in bad places. For example, the choice to leave home at fifteen put me on the highway hitchhiking all over the United States.

If I would have stayed home, I would have been in college by the time I was seventeen. Instead, I didn't go to college until I was forty. The choice I made to use drugs when I was young made my life go in the wrong direction.

WHAT IF?

Stacy, in the story above, decided at age forty to go back to college or high school. She used WHAT IF to move her into action beyond the bad choices of her past. It is never too late to go back to college. Community colleges are very inexpensive and easy to enroll in. It is never too late to finish high school, learn a new skill, attend college. WHAT IF it is truly never too late?

The prison of higher education

After high school graduation, some U.S. youth attend college or universities rather than starting work in a fulltime career.

The reasons for attending additional schooling are different. Some students do not have any idea what career or job to pursue. Enrolling in school buys them time to figure things out. Maybe their parents support a specific goal or career. Parents might "force" their child to attend college to avoid having them live at home, watching too many video games or eating fast food.

There are many reasons that college campuses fill up with young adults. And the students need to jump through a lot of hoops before they can graduate.

Some college campuses are isolated from a main city center. Those students might feel trapped. There is a dress code at many of these institutions of higher learning. Students must attend a predetermined set of classes that are offered at predetermined days and times. They must earn a specific number of credits.

Some students sneak out to drink a beer or have a smoke. They eat terrible food at predetermined and rigidly set hours in a mess hall. The canned food dished out onto plastic bowls and placed on worn trays is unhealthy and unappetizing. They have a tiny cot on which they sleep. The showers are often large rooms with wet floors seething with fungus.

Many of the students have entry-level, minimum wage jobs in addition to the academic requirement. Most of them are broke, tired, anxious, and look forward to graduation. Many have school loans at the end of their sentence. Loan payments might span over 30 years.

Basically, the entire student body is held captive by an unbending administration that holds a thick rulebook over their heads. They essentially become sentenced to four years of academic imprisonment when they choose higher education.

How would you feel about incarceration if you believed that it was a laboratory in which you could experiment with personal change goals? How would you feel about incarceration if the only safe place was behind the prison walls? Undoubtedly, your spirits would lift and your energy would increase.

The Difference Between Prison and Work
An anonymous e-mail

In Prison: You spend the majority of your time in a 10x10 cell.
At Work: You spend the majority of your time in an 8x8 cubicle.

In Prison: You get 3 meals a day.
At Work: You get 1 break a day and have to pay for it.

In Prison: You get time off for good behavior.
At Work: You get more work for good behavior.

In Prison: The guard locks and unlocks the doors for you.
At Work: You must often carry a security card and open all the doors yourself.

In Prison: You can watch TV and play games.
At Work: You get sacked for the above.

In Prison: You get your own toilet.
At Work: You share a toilet with co-workers and strangers.

In Prison: They allow your friends and family to visit.
At Work: You aren't supposed to speak to your family, even by phone.

In Prison: All expenses are paid by the taxpayer with no work required.
At Work: You get to pay all your expenses to work and they deduct taxes from your salary to pay for prisoners.

In Prison: You spend most of your time behind bars wanting to get out.
At Work: You spend most of your time wanting to get out and go inside bars.

In Prison: You deal with wardens.
At Work: They are called managers.

WHAT IF?

What if there was a crystal ball that revealed that you would meet an untimely death by means of a city bus? But luckily, you were arrested instead. You were spared from death and given an opportunity to live on earth for many more years. It's true that you are behind a wall. But isn't it better to be alive? Try to appreciate simple pleasures like a friendly smile or a completion of a task.

Being behind a wall still allows you the possibility for a happier life than many of the "free" people. You can create a life of integrity and personal empowerment.

Words from GOGI Girl Sheila W.

People Pleasing.... Part of my recovery is not that I never people please, but that I know when I am doing it & I am doing it less! My low self-esteem was revealed in the way I would say what I felt you wanted to hear, do what you wanted to do, go where you wanted to go. For years I missed me.

For years, I missed my life because I was preoccupied with other people. And, I wasn't honest. I hated being that way but I wouldn't admit it. Now, I see that my guilt around my addiction led me into this sick cycle and my recovery is taking me out of it. Today, I say, "I don't want to go," and "I don't agree with what you are saying," and even "I refuse to do that."

My dignity is being discovered in my straight-forwardness. God, may I have the courage to share my true feelings...

Your REAL Job

What if your "job" on the inside is to educate and empower others through your examples? You will return to society so fortified, and so solid that nothing and no one can shake you.

What if you are a force for good just waiting to happen? WHAT IF?

This is what I see each and every time I enter a jail or prison. I see women and men who are possibly better at educating at-risk and incarcerated individuals than those who get paid to educate them.

I see women and men who could easily be trained to be social workers, psychologists, teachers, coaches, and leaders. They could be teaching and guiding other people to stop making the same mistakes.

Sadly, I also see hugely influential individuals sitting in the yard, bored beyond all reasonable levels of boredom. They seem to be uninspired and drained of creativity. I think of the promise that their experiences hold. I think of the good that they can and should do.

Art by
Natalie H.

What if their "job," their "task," their "mission" and their "rehabilitation requirements" was to just keep 3 individuals from heading down the slippery slope?

What if we used our weaknesses and made them our finest strengths?

WHAT IF?

- Coach Taylor

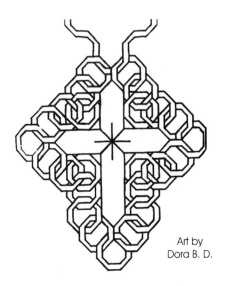

Art by
Dora B. D.

Sketch of Coach Taylor
by Chris H.

Pencil sketch by
GOGI Girl Stephanie R.

Art by
Davida M.

"Live each day to the Fullest!"
—By Liliana R.

An inmate made the following assessment a few months ago during one large GOGI class. She said that she was not able to be "free" on the outside. It was only after she was locked up that she found internal freedom.

How we choose to see something is the determining factor in our experiences. Perception is everything. This is what makes WHAT IF? so powerful. What you choose to notice and do in your life speaks volumes of the individual that you choose to be.

Words from GOGI Girl Wendy R.

I often think of what if there was no GOGI Campus. I would have never had the chance to experience internal freedom and meet the most powerful woman I know today. Thank you, Coach Taylor, for having a dream to help us find our dreams.

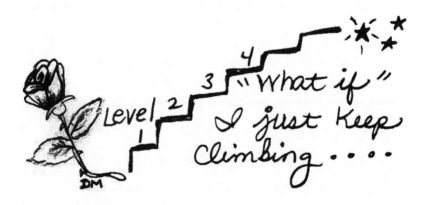

Safe On The Inside

One boy I "coached" spent most of his life in long or short-term "visits" to almost every Juvenile Justice Department facility in Los Angeles.

The other day, his worried mother called me because he was arrested, again. She wanted my advice. Her son was involved in a car accident when he had been driving drunk.

A strange part of me – in fact, nearly all of me – was very grateful that he was locked up. He had been spinning out of control for months. It was only a matter of time before I got a call that he had met the wrong side of a bullet.

While he sits in County awaiting the first in a long series of court sessions, he is undoubtedly discouraged and probably pissed off. He might feel rage and blame everyone but himself.

Me? I am grateful. I am happy that he is locked up. No one was killed. No guns were fired. And, he is safe – from himself.

WHAT IF? behind bars for a while is the only way to keep him alive?

WHAT IF? your incarceration is really an opportunity for you? Could it permit you to live a long and productive life?

Coach Taylor

Words from GOGI Girl Paula B.

I cannot change the past but I can make the future better by concentrating on what I can do now.

While some inmates humbly nodded with understanding, others scoffed at her statement. They remarked that there is nothing good that could come from being locked behind bars. And, how could anything good happen? After all, their families need food, bills paid, and work that needs to be done.

As a matter of fact, the scoffing individuals had legitimate reasons to hold onto their perceptions. However, they were not free from the confines of their perception. It does not take freedom to be free. And being physically "free" does not guarantee freedom.

Words from GOGI Girl Deanna H.

A Woman's Worth

A woman's worth is to overcome her mistakes. To gain back her respect and to give herself that second chance at life.

To ask God to forgive her for all other sins and make amends to him and sisters and brothers and mothers and fathers.

Having our glory, but live to tell the whole story. To have soundness of mind and continue to be kind.

Yes, I committed a crime, but I've done my time and gained back my sincerity, my serenity and now I know my priorities.

My priorities are: To put my family first. To gain back my self-pride. To never give up having the durability and capability of accomplishing my goals — my sense of worth, my sense of being a mother, because to my children I will be one like no other, and I will no longer be a burden to society.

THE TOOL OF "WHAT IF?" will:

- Help you see previously overlooked perspectives and possibilities. You will look at every challenge, every event, every opinion, every reaction, and every action in a different way.

- Help you think new thoughts about new possibilities. You will be empowered with data accumulated through your willingness to consider options.

- Help you take actions based on the new thoughts and possibilities. You will see how others approach similar situations. You will be able to build competencies through the examples of others.

- Help you break old habits and replace them with ones that are more successful. You will be willing to develop new neurological pathways leading to new habits.

Words from GOGI Girl Shannon S.

What GOGI and Coach Taylor means to me is the belief of knowing something in my heart can now be made possible in my head and in my life.

As long as I apply these tools for a new way of thinking and decision making, a new way of life filled with hopes and dreams can only follow.

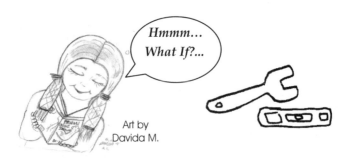

Hmmm... What If?...

Art by Davida M.

THE TRUTH IS. . .

WHAT IF? allows you to see things in a new way.
You will be empowered to see options and
opportunities that others fail to see.
WHAT IF? places you in an immediate position
of self-empowerment because you will see the
many options that you really have
— even in the most difficult situations.
WHAT IF? helps you make SMARTER, STRONGER
decisions because you will see
other points of view and other options.

My Beautiful Child

What's going on with my beautiful child
While her addict mother is out running wild
I'm not there when she says her prayers at night
Or, when she is scared, to hold her tight.
I'm not the one who's holding her hand
And saying "Don't cry baby. I understand."
When she has a problem, where does she go?
Isn't that something that a mother should know?!
How could I walk through my life and not see?
I believed my addiction was only hurting me
At least I could run and hide behind dope.
But my poor baby girl had no choice but to cope.
Now I'm on the road to recovery
I took the first step for her
I'm taking the rest for me.
GOGI is leading her mother back home
Never again will either of us be all alone
I'll have GOGI and she'll have me
That's the way God meant it to be.
- *GOGI Girl Teri, GOGI Campus 2008*

Words from GOGI Girl Deanna H.

Roses are red,
violets are blue.
And for all of
you who are
seeking recovery
& willing to learn
new tools in life,
GOGI is for you too!

Art by
Deanna H.

GOGI Girl Deanna H. and Family.

Words from a little GOGI Girl...

The Rainbow Poem

Pink is for the seconds in a minute
   Yellow is for all the minutes in an hour
Orange is for all the hours in a day
   Red is for all of the days in a week
Blue is for all of the weeks in a month
   Purple is for all the months in a year
Green is for all the years in a decade
   Brown is for all the decades in a century
            The colors of my rainbow is for all
               the centuries from forever that will soon
            come to an end for all of the suffering
               that will end when you experience
            the GOGI Program like my mommy.

--Vontavia H., daughter of GOGI Girl Deanna H.

HOW WHAT IF? WORKS

WHAT IF? is the practice of looking at any situation from an different seat in the theater of life. There might be 200 individuals in a movie theater. The person in each seat generates a slightly different perception. There are alternate realities and other available options.

WHAT IF? is a question that you ask yourself continually. Willingness to let go of your deep-rooted opinions permits the expansion of ideas and awareness.

As you assume WHAT IF? your brain is open to new neurological pathways. These are potential truths from which you can create thoughts and actions. You shift towards a new reality that has accessible options. With What IF? you are able to pull your thoughts away from old habits or patterns.

Coach Taylor outside a prison in Romania.

ADDED BENEFITS OF WHAT IF?

Consider the WHAT IF? option in every situation. There is an additional benefit to asking yourself "WHAT IF?" Anger will not come as quickly with your newfound flexibility. You are more likely to get along better with others and have improved relationships.

YEAH
COACH.
WE LOVE YOU campus
-Laura W. & GOGi

WHY WHAT IF? WORKS...

Your reactions are often based on the actions of others. Your reactions are no longer automatic when you realize that you have options. You are inclined to think before you react if you have choices.

There may be a huge difference in the outcome of events by taking a pause before actions. Asking WHAT IF? generates a "pause" that permits you to consider options.

To a large extent, you can model behaviors until they become habits. Ask yourself, "WHAT IF? I was a calm person, how would I breathe?" "WHAT IF? I was lucky, how would I speak?' "WHAT IF I was very successful, how would I carry myself?"

PUTTING <u>WHAT IF?</u> INTO PRACTICE

You can control your actions if you can control your thoughts. An easy tool for controlling thoughts is to think about how another person might perceive the same situation.

Words from GOGI Girl Laura W.
2008 GOGI Campus Class President

I have learned how to...
Love without conditions
Care without expectations
Feel without fear
Say "No" without guilt
Say "Yes" without compassion
- And to -
Just be without having to DO.

Straight A Students

I worked with a group of 5th grade boys and girls attending a Watts, California, area elementary school. The GOGI team of coaches and I taught the GETTING OUT BY GOING IN concepts for self-empowerment and solid decision-making skills.

Several kids at the school were labeled as having behavioral problems. Both the teachers and parents gave quick approval for the kids to spend time with a "behavioral coach."

I used the WHAT IF? question one day when the group of rowdy 5th graders was particularly uncooperative. I asked "WHAT IF? you were all 'A' students? How would you be behaving right now?"

They quickly sat up straight, clasped their hands and became extraordinarily quiet.

I asked them "So, you would choose to sit straight and at attention if you were all straight 'A' students?"

They nodded in reply.

"I bet it feels pretty cool to be 'A' students?" I asked. They all smiled. The boys and girls made a choice to change their behavior. The new behavior was contrary to the labels that were given to them throughout the school system. They were able to test out new ways of being and behaving when presented with "WHAT IF?"

Coach Taylor

"What IF
I went to College?"
By Davida M.

As simple as it seems, asking yourself the WHAT IF? is likely to transform your actions and reactions in just about every situation. Here are the simple steps to the WHAT IF?

STEP 1) INCOMING INFORMATION - Incoming information can be processed in many different ways. Every piece of information is automatically assigned a meaning from habit. How the information is processed is determined by our attitude, outlook and expectations.

For example, information is processed in unconstructive and unproductive ways if your attitude is negative. As a result, your behavior and reactions are adversely affected. On the other hand, reactions and behavior will be constructive and confident if the information is processed in a positive manner.

Asking the WHAT IF? question allows you to maintain control of your thoughts and how you process information. Control of your thoughts will help you take control of your behavior. What happens when you begin to use the WHAT IF? question? You will experience the incoming information in a new way before you generate a response.

STEP 2) BELLY BREATHING – Breathe the way you were born to breathe - with the entire body involved. This way of breathing buys you time for paying attention to how you respond to events and situations. It also sends oxygen to your brain that permits you to think smartly. When you breathe properly, you can relax more. You make better decisions when you are relaxed.

STEP 3) WHAT IF? – If the BOSS OF YOUR BRAIN doesn't get you over an obstacle — or the FIVE SECOND LIGHTSWITCH doesn't quite work — you can start to ask some WHAT IF? questions.

Ask yourself, "If I was headed towards the airport for a Hawaiian vacation with $1,000, how would I react to this current situation? What would I really care about?" Or…"Five years from now, will I still be upset about someone else's reactions? Or…"How would I handle this situation if I was not reliant upon this individual?"

It is powerful to ask the WHAT IF? Questions. It helps you consider different ways to react to situations. WHAT IF? lets the incident stand on its own by taking all the variables out of the equation.

Do not let feelings or emotions become attached to incidents that you experience. Move on to the next step of the WHAT IF? process if they cloud your judgment.

STEP 4) ANOTHER "WHAT IF" - Let's say that the situation is so distressing that there is no way to pull away from your attachments and change a particular meaning.

Ask yourself a dozen WHAT IF? questions, if you need to. Consider as many options as you can. Give some thought to as many different perspectives as you can.

A real common WHAT IF? is "What would Jesus do?" You can substitute Jesus for just about anyone you admire or respect. Another way to capture the "WHAT IF" mentality is to imagine how someone else might respond.

Ask yourself, "If this happened to. . .Mother Teresa. . . Serena Williams. . . Michael Jordan. . . your mentor. . . Your meditation teacher…. ANYONE ELSE.

How would they handle it?" Ask yourself how they would respond, how they would reply, how they might breathe, or how they would think. You will actually feel a different response when you mimic, imitate, or even FAKE someone else's response.

FAKE IT UNTIL YOU MAKE IT HAPPEN...

You may discover that there is an immense value in "faking it until you make it" as you learn new ways of responding to circumstances.

New neurological pathways form new responses when you fake alternative reactions for 21 days. These pathways essentially reinforce new habits.

Faking is the perfect way to create new neural possibilities and permits your body to respond in a desirable way. It allows you to take charge of your body and become the BOSS OF YOUR BRAIN.

Asking the WHAT IF? Question is really a way for you to master the BOSS OF YOUR BRAIN tool. You will control your reality through empowering new perceptions.

THINK ABOUT IT

With a lack of information in events or circumstances, you might make poor decisions or conclusions. You are more empowered to lead than blindly follow if you are aware of all sides of a story or situation.

Consider an instance when you reacted hastily to information before you obtained additional information. Did you understand the perspective better when you were able to listen to another's point of view?

Is it possible that the way you first react to a situation is not necessarily the best response? Is it possible that you might respond differently with supplementary data obtained from asking the WHAT IF questions? Take a moment to reflect on some of your past reactions. Think about the different situations.

How do you think that your Pastor, the Pope, God, your grandmother, a child, Martin Luther King, or ANYONE ELSE would react to the same situation?

What is happening in your life right now? Is the habit of being angry, judgmental, critical, or self-critical serving you in any way? Does this negative habit keep you stuck? Does it have a purpose? Ask yourself some WHAT IF questions and consider some new possibilities.

WHAT IF you were considered to be the calmest individual on the yard? WHAT IF people asked you how you are able to stay calm in the face of chaos? WHAT IF you were the kind of individual who could see many different perspectives simultaneously?

WATCH OTHERS

Art by Natalie H.

Observing others gives you vital information and places you in a powerful position of understanding. Observe someone who is angry. Are they giving themselves enough time to consider other ways of reacting? Are they reacting out of habit? Are they accomplishing their objective with anger? What does their limited perspective tell you about them?

Your observation of others is a powerful tool. You will know more about how they operate. You can assess what behaviors are similar to ones that you want to let go of in favor of finding freedom.

Observe others - truly observe others – from a compassionate stance. You will be further empowered to be the Boss of Your Brain. You will not let habits or old ways of thinking and behaving "run your program" when you are the Boss of Your Brain. There is no law that limits your internal growth. There is no law that regulates how you respond to things.

WHAT IF?

is one of the most powerful tools for opening up the possibilities of new responses and reactions. Asking yourself **WHAT IF?** *will permit you to see the other person's point of view and you are more likely to start effective communication when you understand their motivation.*

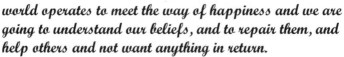

Words from GOGI Girl Aura

To repair our life, we must admit that we have been living our life in disloyalty.

Through GOGI we can learn to trust ourselves and to trust others and have faith to solve our problems.

We need to learn how the world operates to meet the way of happiness and we are going to understand our beliefs, and to repair them, and help others and not want anything in return.

Prove it to yourself. Try it by "writing" down how you want to help others. Write what you want in life and ♥never give up.♥ Always learn from your problems. The secret is to smile and be happy.

Words from GOGI Girl Felicia (Mimi) J.

The Big Question. WHAT IF? What if I never used drugs? What would my life be like without drugs? I now understand WHAT IF taps into my imagination and it becomes an infinite vision. The WHAT IF tool gives me the right to imagine all the possibilities, consider all the options and Boss of My Brain to actually do them and be successful.

The book says WHAT IF is important for anyone who feels trapped, stuck and/or cornered. WHAT IF is a tool which can make any good person better. As an addict, I can experience the feeling of hope. Hope is a huge road to the light at the end of the tunnel.

I have always dreamed of the possibilities of my success. I wonder WHAT IF this or WHAT IF that. Sometimes I would even become jealous and envious of others because I knew that I could do what they were doing. Then bucking authority would be a reaction because I am "just as" educated or capable as them.

WHAT IF is not negative or regretting but it is looking TOWARD the possibilities. Creating a clean start and thinking positive to a new WHAT IF. It is like going beyond to create, call or think or act into existence the WHAT IF POSSIBILITIES OF MY LIFE.

SMILE Always
Wendy R.

WHAT IF?
In Action

MICHELLE GETS FIRED

It took Michelle months to land a job. The only problem is that she does not have respect for her supervisor.

The supervisor shows up late or hung-over, and berates most of the employees, especially Michelle. In fact, Michelle is the only one who got "written up" for infractions that everyone else gets away with.

> "What if I stay calm? How can I turn this around?" by Jennifer B.

Michelle showed up for work after a long weekend, and learned that her boss had fired her. Her supervisor blamed her for everyone else's mistakes and no one defended Michelle.

Michelle was not in a position to be unemployed and finding a job is never an easy task with an ex-felon stamp on your forehead. She did not have any savings and bills were stacked high. The more she thought about how unfair the situation was, the angrier she got.

To let the questions of WHAT IF? work for her, Michelle needed to take control of her thoughts. First, she did BELLY BREATHING to get her body to relax. She knew that she was more intelligent when her body was relaxed.

Then...**WHAT IF? IN ACTION**

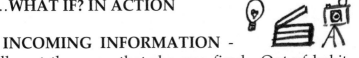

1)   INCOMING INFORMATION - Michelle got the news that she was fired. Out of habit, she automatically got mad at the supervisor. She wanted to tell her side of the story. Being fired meant that she was taking the fall for her supervisor's dishonesty and inability to do a good job. Michelle got angry. Getting angry was not Michelle's most intelligent state of mind.

2) BREATHE - Doing BELLY BREATHING gave Michelle a little more time to take control of her thoughts and actions. Breathing helped her process information intelligently. Michelle began to breathe and let her entire body relax. She considers some of her options: BOSS OF YOUR BRAIN and FIVE SECOND LIGHTSWITCH are tools she can use. In this case, however, she decides WHAT IF? will work to empower her and get her on the path that she has set for herself.

3) WHAT IF? - Once Michelle had taken a breath, she asked herself, "If I had a pocket full of cash, how would I react? What if my next job is just waiting for me?" With a little emotional distance, Michelle realized that she would eventually get another job. She was relieved that she would no longer work for her unsupportive supervisor.

4) ANOTHER WHAT IF? - Let's say that the situation is very disturbing. Not even the idea of a quick job helps Michelle see things differently. Michelle then looks fast-forward into her life. Thinking to herself, "I know that I'm going to get work somewhere else. WHAT IF? I had the new job right now?

How would I feel? How would someone else handle getting fired? What are other ways for me to handle the situation?"Michelle continues to consider possibilities.

What if this situation happened to Martin Luther King.. ..Jesus. . .the Buddha.. ...ANYONE ELSE...

How would they handle the situation?" She wondered, "How would God react? Coach Taylor? Or even Homer Simpson?"

The answer will be clear if Michelle asks this question while breathing fully. This job is just a job. She had jobs in the past and she will have jobs in the future. Future jobs are likely to be more supportive of her talents

Art by Davida M.

and skills. Being out of a job is inconvenient because of financial challenges. But she will immediately look for a job that better fits her skills.

When Michelle chooses to mimic, imitate, and even FAKE how someone else might respond she feels very differently about the situation. She is more objective and less angry.

WHY IT WORKS

Asking the WHAT IF? questions works because it gives you the power over habits and automatic responses.

Art by Davida M.

OBSERVE OTHERS...

This week your challenge is to notice how people react. Are they automatically reacting, or are they considering different options before they respond? Do they breathe before reacting or is the reaction rapid and without much thought?

Also, observe yourself...

What happens when you practice the WHAT IF? question in your daily routine? Under what situations is it difficult? When is it easy to consider options of acting and reacting?

Art by Taylor W.

Words from GOGI Girl Margie B.

Becoming a GOGI Coach

I believe that I can help women by sharing my experience about my past and to be supportive to them by helping them understand their past and how they can become their own coach.

I also want to share with them how the GOGI book taught me to cope with my past and that I'm not alone.

There are people out in the world that want to help you. And help them be stronger and more positive with themselves and with others.

U MATTER

...OH U MATTER...
To U who wears a smile and to U who wears a frown
To U whose home is a warm bed and to
U whose home is the cold ground
To U who sees yourself as fat and to
U who sees yourself as too thin
To U who judges myself and others by the color of our skin

...OH U MATTER...
To U who lives it up wealthy rich and to
U who lives it down dirt poor
To U who takes a stand for peaceful and to
U who takes the side of war
To U with mental illness and to U whose mind is well
To U whose god is stillness and to U whose heaven is hell

...OH U MATTER...
U really make a difference to me in U'r own way
U really do contribute something good everyday
Don't ever underestimate the difference
U make in U'r own way
In U'r own way

...OH U MATTER...
To U who wants to die and to U who's dying to live
To U who shares to much and to U who cannot give
To U whose world is gay and to U who keeps it strait
To U who lives to love and to U who loves to hate

...OH U MATTER...
U really make a difference to me in U'r own way
U really do contribute something good everyday
Don't ever underestimate the difference
U make in U'r own way

--Composition By: Stefana Dadas ©2000

Art by Davida M,

TOOLS FOR THE SPIRIT

Sketch of
Coach
Taylor by
Laura A.

Thank you S.G.I.

Art by
JackiLyn S.

& Coach Taylor ♡

Words from GOGI Girl Amber H.

Confined

No choice but to deal with me.
Nothing left to do besides
deal with my reality...
So, I can really see.
Why do it differently this time...
Not just my physical freedom.

**EVERYTHING THAT DEFINES MY LIFE
IS ON THE LINE!**

Confined

To face me, my choices
And not only how those choices
Have affected me...but most importantly
THOSE WHO TRULY LOVE ME!
My child suffers because
I CHOSE to act so selfishly.
Consumed with so many emotions
I only wanted and chose to numb them.
Instead of easing the pain,
I prolonged it and spread it out
Like a disease.
So, Father God had no choice, but to confine me!
So, I could really see.
He's shown me what WAS, IS, and
WHAT COULD BE.
As a promise to him and my Baby Girl,
THIS TIME I CHOOSE ME!

CHAPTER 8

POSITIVE TWA

POSITIVE THOUGHTS, WORDS, ACTIONS

A recent scientific study conducted by the University of Michigan explored "Positive Attitude," as it relates to human growth and success. They invested a great deal of time and resources and came up with an obvious result. They found a correlation, or a link, between having a positive attitude and experiencing positive outcomes.

It may seem like common sense, but very few of us actually focus on the positive things in our life. However, most people agree that looking at the "brighter side" of life is important.

Positive Thoughts, Words and Actions offer positive results, even if it is only in your positive perception or positive experience of negative stimuli.

With relationships, you are happier when positive attributes are your focus — even if the other person never changes!

Think about it. How much of your thinking, words, and actions are negative? Are they negative because your situation is negative?

Are you reacting negatively and justifying it by the situation? Is the other person wrong? "They" did it?

Are you negative because the world needs to be supportive for you to be positive?

Do things need to be positive around you in order for you to be positive as well? Do you really want to give up control and live in constant reaction to your environment? Or do you want to be the Boss?

Think about the words you use daily. Are they "negative," "positive" or "neutral?"

You might be surprised how many words might fall in the negative category.

Some women have negative viewpoints. Their boyfriend has 101 faults that "make" them unhappy. Their situations keep them from being internally happy. Some women tend to blame their outlook on situations...their partner...their job...the system...anyone but themselves.

Do you really believe the following statements? "I'd be happier if I was at home," or "I'd be happy if I had money," or "I'd be happy if I had a good paying job."

A fundamental truth: Art by Natalie H.

1) **POSITIVE THOUGHTS** - help you start the pathway toward positive living.

2) **POSITIVE WORDS** - your word choice leads to the actions you choose. Your word choice determines your positive or negative outcome.

3) **POSITIVE ACTIONS** - your actions are a result of your thoughts and your words. Your actions broadcast who you are to the world and what you are thinking.

Where do we start?

Art by Davida M,

Everyone has unique positive traits. What are yours? Are you patient? Enthusiastic? Loyal? Peaceful?

Ask someone close to you for help in identifying positive traits. What are YOUR three best qualities? What are THEIR three best qualities?

What if you were to focus on three of your best qualities regularly? Your three best qualities will help you with your Thoughts, Words and Actions. POSITIVE TWA – Positive Thoughts, Words, Actions will come out of your focus on what is right, not what is wrong.

POSITIVE TWA allows you to use techniques proven by scientists and human behaviorists.

> ℘ Positive thoughts precede a
> Positive life experience. ℘

Positive thoughts lead directly to positive words. It is difficult to be negative when you are thinking positive thoughts. The two are linked. Positive words lead to positive actions. Positive actions broadcast who you are to the world.

Try this...

When you have a negative thought, you can use the tools you have learned in this book. Try the Five Second Lightswitch and swap the thought with a positive thought. Give the thought five seconds and then swap it out with a positive one.

"Yeah, it really sucks I have to go into work an hour earlier every day. That really cuts into my meditation time. I like meditating and we don't do anything the first hour, anyway," is how the thought pattern might go.

After five seconds of entertaining how terrible things are, swap it out with something like, "I am grateful and I like my job, I will actually get more done, it is likely that I will get off early, and no one is around that early so it will be peaceful. I can make this into a good thing for myself."

Make certain that you are headed toward a more positive experience for every negative thought. "Another mail call and there's nothing for me. No one cares," might be the reaction to an empty mailbag. Get three positive thoughts into your head as quickly as possible.

"OK, so I received no letters. I guess I am not writing enough letters to the right people. But, I am sleeping better than before." Any three positive thoughts will turn the tide toward positive words and positive actions.

By doing so, you are likely to be more successful, healthier, and have better relationships. You will be happier when you get in the habit of replacing negative thoughts with a surplus of positive thoughts.

Use POSITIVE TWA towards creating a positive experience, regardless of what is going on around you. Positive THOUGHTS, WORDS and ACTIONS empower you to be the best that you can be. POSITIVE TWA – POSITIVE THOUGHTS, WORDS, AND ACTIONS.

POSITIVE TWA will help you:

- Remain positive about life regardless of the circumstance.
- Focus on your key positive traits and outnumber the negatives with positives.
- Create more opportunities to move forward in your life.

THE TRUTH IS. . .

POSITIVE TWA *allows you to balance your thoughts, words and actions so that there are more positive events than negative.*

POSITIVE TWA *reminds you to consider your positive qualities and trains your mind to look for the positive in situations.*

POSITIVE TWA *is based on the fact that positive thoughts create the perceptual experience of positive experiences.*

(THOUGHTS, WORDS, ACTIONS)
TWA *are three keys that allows you to control your thoughts, word, and actions.*

Words from GOGI Girl Adrianne K.

In and out, in and out of jails and prison I would go. Over and over. GOGI has interrupted that pattern that I was so used to following. I have made so many promises to my aunt. Every time I would parole she would get so excited about my return home. ⟨ be so strong while standing by just to watch me stay out a few months and soon return to jail again.

GOGI Girl Adrianne K.

I'm proud to say that I won't be returning to jail and disappointing her again. This time I'm taking my GOGI tools with me.

GOGI Girl Adrianne K. & Family

This time I will be the Boss of my Brain. I will take control of my life.

Because of GOGI, I will earn my aunt's trust.

Because of my GOGI tools, I will gain my aunt's trust.

HOW DOES POSITIVE TWA WORK?

POSITIVE TWA works on the premise that positive thoughts inspire positive words that create positive actions.

HERE'S WHY POSITIVE TWA WORKS...

Negative thoughts bathe your entire neurological system with negativity. Every cell of your body is receiving negative impulses much like being in a room with bad music blaring. Your body cannot escape the ramifications of negative (and positive) thought.

After you generate a thought, it leads to words. Unconstructive words filter throughout your body's neurology. The negative thoughts travel from your brain, through your body, out of your mouth and into the environment.

Negativity operates much like a radio signal and sends vibrations into the space around you. Basically, your ears hear those negative words when you talk trash about a person or a situation. The negativity permeates every cell of your body, bathing you with negative messages, even when you are talking about someone else!

Negativity filters deep into every cell of your body and experiences feelings from the words you generated.

For example, your entire body turns into one big bundle of negative energy when you are cussing at a custody assistant who tells you to go into your cell because he did not like how you wore your shirt. You, rather than he, pay the bigger price of your negative reaction. He may not like what you say and may write you up, but every cell of your body is in negative vibration.

Your thoughts are negative, your words are negative and your actions are negative. You lose.

Everyone experiences your negativity when you are upset and react in a negative way, but no one experiences it more profoundly than you do. The good news is that research suggests that positive thoughts are more powerful than negative thoughts.

With positive thoughts, we can outweigh the impact of negativity easily. With enough practice, we can outweigh negativity effortlessly and automatically.

There are some women who barely see negativity. They focus beyond the negative into what is inherently positive about their life. For these women it does not take a place or a paycheck for internal freedom to occur.

POSITIVE TWA is a tool for you. Internal freedom is within your reach with POSITIVE TWA.

Words from GOGI Girl Christina H.

I'm learning that the more information (good info) I receive helps me on my journey, the stronger I feel. Letting go of old feelings is something I really need to work on, to move on. Closing the door on the past is a very different thing for me.

But one thing I have been able to do is take responsibility for my actions. I found that when I share my recovery time and how I was able to abstain from using and going to all those places that did not honor me; I found this made me feel good.

When a person approached me to let me know that I touched them in some way through what I shared, the feeling I got was great.

Words from GOGI Girl Liliana R.
Life doesn't frighten me anymore. GOGI has taught me
to deal with my problems and confront them head on.
Life will not always be full of joy and happiness, but it's
the way I react to life's problems and disappointments
that will make a difference in my life.
Life can either make me or break me. Today I choose to
live life to the fullest and make my dreams a reality.

Art by Davida M.

Words from GOGI Girl Deanna H.

What the GOGI programs means to me is that I
will not be leaving the women's jail as just another
inmate. I will be leaving as a successful inmate. I
will have values, morals, goals, serenity, honesty,
purity, humility, gratitude, love, joy, faith,
patience, tolerance, etc.

I will leave here with a reason to want to do
something positive with my life and to be
somebody. A reason to be a good mother to my
children.

A reason for not giving up, but to start over new.

A reason to appreciate my higher power and not
to go off of my own understanding.

This program helps me to respect and obey the
law, no matter what. And to know that God has a
purpose for all of us and we need to soul search
and find that purpose and fulfill it.

100 Good Things…

I conducted my own mini-experiment one day at a youth prison. I gave each girl one of those $2.00 composition notebooks and a pencil. Their assignment was to write down 100 good things about themselves.

"I ain't got 100 good things about me, coach," Laura responded.

"Do you brush your teeth?" I asked.

"Of course," she replied.

"Well, that is one really good thing about you, Laura. You brush your teeth. Write that down as the number one."

The lists were interesting and revealing. "I kiss good," "I like music," and "I like sports" were often sandwiched between "my sister likes me" and "I am a good *friend.*"

Eventually, each of the girls completed their list of 100 good qualities. Of that list of 100, they were to identify personal traits that they believed were their most important ones.

"I am a good friend," "I love my family" and "I am athletic," ranked among the most popular. "I am committed, loyal and dedicated" occasionally popped up in a few lists.

The girls realized that they had many good qualities. They were empowered to rely on these good qualities throughout their day. The idea was to identify with something positive about yourself and use it when unproductive habits surface.

You can do the same.

Coach Taylor

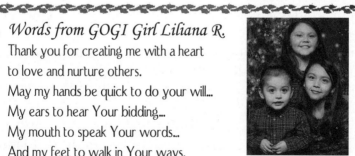

Words from GOGI Girl Liliana R.

Thank you for creating me with a heart
to love and nurture others.
May my hands be quick to do your will…
My ears to hear Your bidding…
My mouth to speak Your words…
And my feet to walk in Your ways.
Amen

*GOGI Girl Liliana R.'s Kids :
Hennessy, Michael & Destinee*

With so many negatives around you, it is not easy to expect a positive outcome. It may seem very difficult to find anything positive in what appears to be a terribly bad situation. In truth, bad situations are saddening, maddening, discouraging and depressing.

Regardless of whether the situation changes or not, if we maintain positive TWA, positive THOUGHTS, WORDS and ACTIONS, our experience of the situation will be more tolerable.

Again, even if our situation does not change, the experience of our situation will become more tolerable when we CHOOSE POSITIVE TWA.

Where is the positive?

What could be good about getting fired? Divorced? A loved one's death? There may be nothing positive, but how we choose to experience the negative is what is critical. Deep within ourselves, we can remain positive within a sea of negative. We find our own tiny morsel of goodness.

Sometimes the positive is not as hidden as we originally thought. What could be good about getting fired? Besides the "routine" of the daily workday, you might start another employment and discover new opportunities. You might earn better pay. You might meet new people or find a new friend. You might get more enjoyment and less stress at the next job. What could be good about getting a divorce? There is a chance that you will fall in love again and have an opportunity to build something better.

There is an opportunity to look within and take responsibility for yourself and not default to blaming your partner. You can't blame someone who is no longer a variable in your blame game.

What is good about the death of a loved one? You could focus on fond memories from your experiences together. You learn to value life. You learn to seize each moment as if it were the last. You learn to love more deeply.

What is good about being locked up? Well…it depends on the direction of your focus. You have the opportunity to restructure your entire way of thinking, being, and reacting.

You can share learning with others. You can expand your perception of right and wrong. You can build a strategy for internal bliss.

You can meditate, work out, work, study new subjects, read and become very literate, crochet, write, and do lots of thinking about life's possibilities.

Internal freedom is within reach if you can distance yourself from the negative and fill every day with POSITIVE TWA while you are locked up.

Positive breeds positive $(+ = +)$

Those around you will have a positive experience when you verbalize positive words and every cell of your body reverberates with POSITIVE TWA. When you focus on POSITIVE TWA, it is highly probable that you will experience increasingly positive outcomes.

What we believe to be important today, including what really upsets us, is likely to have less importance tomorrow. Is it really worth being negative?

Children may lose their temper over not getting something they want, but within a few minutes, their attention is elsewhere. They move on to something else that is just as important.

Words from GOGI Girl Zel O.

How can my services help others since I've been a GOGI girl? I can honestly say it has been a blessing being placed here. I used to be in the dark but now can see this is where I needed to be. I can now share everything I have learned with others, things like anger, character, unhappiness, non-caring, guilt, this program has done me a lot of good. "A True Blessing."

The best word to sum it up is "Awesome" and it keeps getting better. I'll be going home soon but I have a plan to stay in contact with Coach Taylor. She is such an inspiration to me.

Words from GOGI Girl Kim H.

The sun is shining on a new day
I wake up and say,
Good Morning to me!
It's safe to be
who I am today
A GOGI girl!
Today is a good day
because I have a better way
to deal with my pain
and the strain of life
Now I choose to use
my GOGI tools
and follow NEW rules
on this path
called life!
I've opened my eyes
And I realize
That opportunity
Is my new reality...
all thanks to GOGI!

Words from GOGI Girl Liliana R.
GOGI, My New Way of Life

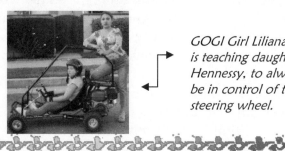

My heart was shattered, broken
down and to the curb
To face society, I no longer had
the nerve
　I felt defeated, so much hurt and
　so much pain
　My eyes were swollen; tears kept
　falling like the rain
I felt a failure as a mother and so much shame
My son is adopted due to drugs and I'm to blame
　Each day when I awoke, I felt such sorrow
　Please take me Lord; I don't want to live
　to see tomorrow
I had no goals, no inspirations, or dreams in life
My life was filled with hurt, shame, misery and strife
　I got arrested and for a minute started stressing
　But I found GOGI, and Oh My God was that a blessing
I've learned forgiveness, how to feel and how to trust
Let go of guilt, forgave myself, found peace at last
With GOGI tools, I no longer need a blast
　With GOGI girls, I get support that's like no other
　I'm not alone, we laugh, we cry, we have each other
Abstained from drugs, I now have dreams & inspirations.
I've learned with GOGI how to handle situations.

GOGI Girl Liliana R. pictured above with son Michael and future GOGI Coach Magdalena.

GOGI Girl Liliana R. is teaching daughter, Hennessy, to always be in control of the steering wheel.

An inmate may be stuck in the despair of their current situation. "Woe is me, I am locked up. My husband left me and my kid is in Juvi," can be moved closer to, "I can control my TWA. I cannot control my husband's departure. I cannot control my son's behavior. But I can be a positive force for everyone in my unit. I can be healthier and happier than I was yesterday. I can be positive and pray that my ex-husband and my son run into positive people like me."

Moving beyond a negative outlook leads to seeing positive aspects of a situation. Women who master TWA look and speak positively. They look toward change and have a far better chance of recovering from a relapse than their negative counterparts.

Positive women recover speedily because they do not wallow in what might be wrong with situations. They move towards the direction of possibilities. They push forward and with a positive approach regardless of any previous failures.

Women inmates who accept their situation and who "get on with their life" have a tendency to do far better than those who harbor ill feelings about past events or behavior.

Is it a sign of weakness to be positive? There are some women who feel that they are "selling out" if they are positive. They think that they appear "soft" if they let go of anger or do good for others. Some women believe that it is a sign of weakness to learn or simplify and go with their lives. Some women perceive positive outlooks as being weak. However, they mistakenly use negativity as a coping tool.

Negative women are also prone to relapse and have a lower rate of breaking old and unproductive habits. They are limiting their internal freedom. Positive people recover more quickly.

Use your time as a powerful period of self-reflection and you will see that positive qualities are signs of strength.

Positive Attitude, Positive Thinking, Positive Talking

Women inmates with positive thoughts, positive words, and positive actions and a wide group of positive acquaintances tend to cope better. They hold positive qualities during incarceration and also when they return home to their families.

Positive direction is momentum that permits individuals to do far better than others. They set goals and are successful in reaching them. The secret of goal setting is not to let failures or mistakes obstruct your goal. Move toward the goal regardless of any setback. Ten steps forward and two steps back is, in reality, eight steps ahead.

Goal setters usually have multiple goals and don't toss out goals because they "failed" to do everything exactly right. They know that they can learn from setbacks. One goal might be to read one book every month. or learn another language. Working out or meditating three times a week is a goal. Each goal is different.

If your entire "world" rides on one change or goal, it might be devastating when the natural process of change does not meet personal linear expectations. Change is like a dance with forward and backwards movement. Ten steps forward and two steps back is still...eight steps ahead of where you were.

◊ Self-Esteem ◊

◊ Many incarcerated women ask me how they can increase their self-esteem when they see themselves as incarcerated drug addicts with a long history of abuse and failure. How we feel about ourselves is first a result of how our parents and our family treat us, but there comes a point when we can take control and we can begin to develop our self esteem as we want it to be.

Self-esteem comes through esteemable acts. No matter how many times you have been abused, no matter how many drugs you have taken, no matter how much harm you have caused yourself and others, you can begin today to build self-esteem. You do this through the choices of today. Esteemable acts increase your self esteem.

What is an esteemable act? Seeing a piece of trash on a table and tossing it in the trash. An esteemable act is smiling at someone even when you know they will not smile back. An esteemable act is keeping your room clean, keeping your body clean, reading a book, lending a hand, offering to serve, volunteering to assist, listening when you would rather talk, walking beyond an argument, saying I am sorry, saying I understand, saying I respect you, saying I forgive you, saying I forgive myself.

Esteemable acts are those which promote harmony. Esteemable acts are those which come from the heart, not the defenses. Esteemable acts are those where gratitude and humility are at the forefront of the motivation.

Each of us has the opportunity right now to find one small esteemable act. With enough of these small acts we suddenly find we have nurtured and earned a solid self esteem.

No matter how badly you may have been treated by family or life, your self-esteem is there for you to build. Begin now. Find an esteemable act. Begin the process of growing and learning beyond your circumstance. ◊

Coach

HOW TO MASTER <u>POSITIVE TWA</u>

STEP 1) AWARENESS – Take a moment to imagine what it would be like if you controlled your internal world to such an extent that you were perpetually positive.

Art by Natalie H.

Become acutely aware of when you are positive and when you are negative. The fact is, you cannot think positively and speak negatively at the same time. You cannot speak negatively and have positive actions at the same time.

Repeated thoughts, words and actions become well-worn neurological habits. The well-worn neurological habits bypass conscious thought and become an intuitive automatic reaction. Become aware of what you think, what words you use, and the actions you take and change will be lasting. Become aware of what others hear you say and how they might interpret your communication. With AWARENESS you are on your way to escaping the "auto pilot" cycle of negativity.

STEP 2) PAUSE *BEFORE* YOU SPEAK - Before you say anything, pause and consider the thoughts, words and actions that you are about to choose.

Words pop into your mind as thoughts before you say them. Take charge of the thoughts and demand that they get reformulated, morphed, modified, changed, or swapped into positive words.

Pause before you speak and pause before you respond. Take in feedback from others about the words that you have chosen. How are people responding to your positive, or negative, words and actions?

Think about those women who say they "are only speaking the truth." Perhaps they should consider how much of their communication is actually the truth and

> **"He's such an idiot," is just as truthful as "He's acted smarter before."**
> **Coach Taylor**

then focus on the message of their words. Do you really need to point out the entire negative? Does it really do any good to complain and point out flaws? Consider that your negative "truth" is really just your negative experience or opinion. Your truth is not necessarily their truth. Will your negative thoughts, words and actions "change" them? Unlikely.

There might be a guard who is a jerk most of the time. You can say that he is a jerk. You can have negative thoughts, negative words and even negative actions towards this negative guard. You can be caught in his negative loop or you can refocus on someone, something, or some thoughts that are more positive. Take the power out of the other person's hands and claim responsibility for your positive experiences.

STEP 3) SLOW DOWN - Don't rush to think, speak or act. Very few things in life require immediate responses and actions. Most situations in our life would be better managed if we took a bit more time in reacting. There is a popular technique of counting to 10 before you utter a word or engage in an action. Use this technique if it helps.

Your communication becomes purposeful and positive when you slow down. Interestingly enough, people who use pauses and contemplative thought in their lives are often considered to appear "smarter" or "well educated" or "grounded." Slowing down is not automatic and/or reactionary. Slowing down is purposeful and precise.

STEP 4)   OBSERVE - When you speak to someone, watch their reactions. When they speak you can observe their process of thought. Look at the entire exchange of communication. Are your words having the effect you intended? If not, stop talking.

Great
Opportunities
Good
Individuals

Creating
Amazing
Meaningful
Powerful
Unbelievable
Serious

By GOGI Girl Lilian R.

*Self Portrait
By Chris H.*

Art by
Natalie H.

*GOGI Girl Amber O. & Justin
1st GOGI Couple 4-Life*

Words from GOGI Girl Adrienne R.

Why Cry When You Caused It?

Woe is me says the drug addict.

My baby doesn't know me; my family doesn't want me around.

I'm the cause of me not smiling, just a constant frown.

I have no money due to me being unemployed.

I thought it was cool to hang on the block and be one of
the boys.

When I'm in jail I can't call anybody collect.

That's the reality that I must accept.

When I'm out there I'm a star. Locked up you're out of mind,
out of sight, your homies forget who you are.

It's a constant struggle and your head hangs low.

Even more so when your visit doesn't show.

Now you sit on your bunk mad at the world.

Crying because you lost your innocence you had as a little
girl in jail once again for committing a crime

Hurting yourself, those drugs have you lost in time.

Sitting on your rack.

Reflecting on how you can get your life back.

You put in a chaplain request.

Hoping that prayer would give your mind some rest.

Now you read your daily bread.

Thanking God one more time that you're not dead.

You know that resisting the urge is a struggle and a fight.

However, this time you know you will change & make it right.

Or, will you?

Words from GOGI Girl Liliana R.

Anything Is Possible

Life holds no promises as to what will come your way.
You must search for your own ideals and work
toward reaching them.
Life makes no guarantees as to what you'll have.
It just gives you time to make choices and to take chances,
and to discover what secrets might come your way.
If you are willing to take the opportunities
you are given and utilize the abilities you have.
You will constantly fill your life with special moments and
unforgettable times.
No one knows the mysteries of life or its ultimate meaning.
But for those who are willing to believe in their
dreams and in themselves...
Life is a precious gift in which anything is possible.

Words from GOGI Girl Demetri M.

Dear Little Sister, I'm writing you a letter to say a few words. Always trust and believe in God, knowing that He will never put more on you than you can bear.

I've learned in the GOGI program to LET GO, FORGIVE and CLAIM RESPONSIBILITY for my life. So I now BELLY BREATHE, use my SMART THINKING and make better decisions. My POSITIVE THOUGHTS, WORDS AND ACTIONS are key components to my living a productive life.

I am imparting these gifts to you so you might use them well in your life's journey.

Love, Your sister, D. M.

REFLECTION

What words do you use to describe your husband or partner? When you speak to your friends about your mate, are you being critical or complimentary? What about when you talk about your best friend? Your education? What words do you use choose to describe your job? Your meals? Your health? Your family? How do you put into words what you think about your future? Today? Your past? Your parents? Your boss? Your supervisor? Your past mistakes? Prospects for your future?

Focus on areas of your life using POSITIVE TWA. Create positive thoughts, replacing the negative and unproductive opinions and impressions with a focus on positive. Acknowledge three positive things about yourself that you can focus on and emphasize. Choose positive words. Focus on positive actions.

Remember...

Lasting change is generally gradual and occurs over a stretch of time. Change is easier when you become aware of your thoughts. Be attentive to your words. Pause before taking actions.

POSITIVE TWA will strengthen you as you move forward. You can inch your way towards thought, positive talk and note its effect on your choice of actions. POSITIVE TWA leads to positive character, positive experiences with others, and a positive experience in your life.

Art by Liliana R.

WATCH OTHERS

Listen to others. Some people seem to talk as though they are on "auto pilot" and do not think before they speak. Positive talkers are usually more careful in their choice of words. They often speak less and have more control over their thoughts, emotions and words.

You are likely to discover vital information when observing others. Are they positive or negative? You can manage and direct your reactions with positive word choices and see how others succeed by their word choices.

POSITIVE TWA permits you to create the kind of experience that supports your internal freedom. POSITIVE TWA is a powerful tool for freedom before your release.

Words from GOGI Girl Stacy P.
Confusing
My life has been confusing because it seems I am always abusing the things we take for granted.
    My friends and family try diffusing the things I find amusing.
    They say my view is slanted. Since I brought GOGI into my life, I feel no more strife.
    And nothing now has to be recanted.

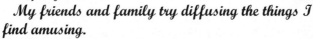

Consider this...
POSITIVE TWA *will keep you aware of your negative and positive thoughts and words.*

POSITIVE TWA *helps put you in the driver's seat and helps you take your thoughts off "auto pilot."*

POSITIVE TWA
In Action

PAT QUITS SMOKING WEED

Pat faced many troubling thoughts when she decided to quit smoking weed. She wanted to be very mindful of her thought patterns. Her thoughts undoubtedly ended up as actions because that is how her human brain works. Every action begins with a thought.

Pat had the idea to have just one hit. This thought created a new thought. "I am such a loser for not being able to quit." The thoughts propelled her into other thoughts. "But it sure smells good," she remembered. "I get so relaxed and it helps me to chill out."

Pat needed to take control and let POSITIVE TWA work for her. She remembered the theory of POSITIVE TWA. She also knew she could use the tool of POSITIVE TWA at any time to take control of her thoughts and behavior.

She knew that her life was up to her no matter how many thoughts flooded her mind. She remembered her POSITIVE personal qualities. Pat took steps to take control over her thoughts and actions.

1) Pat creates her own internal positive attitude. She thinks of the positive aspects in her life. She thinks of her talents. She focuses on her future. The present is going to get her into trouble. The future is where she will find the strength to move forward.

2) Pat has the ability to use the FIVE SECOND LIGHTSWITCH to exchange potentially destructive thinking for positive thinking. She is no longer a slave to her old habits.

3) Pat begins to choose positive words when she thinks about her positive attributes. She CAN and WILL succeed.

> *"I Can – I Will Do It."*
> *- by Jennifer B.*

She knows she has succeeded in the past. She will succeed in the future. She begins to use powerful words like CAN and WILL. These words influence her actions.

WHY POSITIVE TWA WORKS

POSITIVE TWA works on the principal that negative thoughts and words bring negative results — and positive thoughts and words bring positive results and shape POSITIVE TWA you will find an easier path toward success in every area of your life.

The kind of future that you wish for yourself is within reach. You will notice that you have become more powerful when you use TWA.

Use POSITIVE TWA in your communication. Others will begin to react to you more positively. Your positive presence supports change in your surroundings.

OBSERVE YOURSELF AND OTHERS...

Notice that the pace quickens when women respond negatively. Those who are slower to react are more attentive in their responses.

Observe the ratio of negative and positive words that you use. Remember that three POSITIVE thoughts will outweigh one NEGATIVE thought.

Anytime that you think, "I can't," add "but I can do something else." Add "I have accomplished many things but maybe not this one." Say, "I am better off now."

Keep adding positive thoughts. What are your positive qualities?

READ

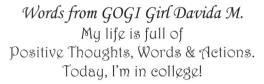

There are tons and tons of books available about the lives of successful women. In each case, you will find that these women are POSITIVE, not negative, about any situation to which they may find themselves. READ, READ, READ biographies, autobiographies, "how-to" books.....anything that supports your POSITIVE TWA.

Words from GOGI Girl Davida M.
My life is full of
Positive Thoughts, Words & Actions.
Today, I'm in college!

♥ Five generations ♥
are saved
by the use
of the
♥ GOGI tools. ♥

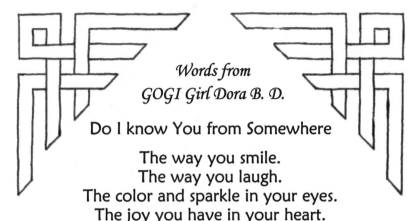

Words from
GOGI Girl Dora B. D.

Do I know You from Somewhere

The way you smile.
The way you laugh.
The color and sparkle in your eyes.
The joy you have in your heart.
The way you show someone you care.
I'm sure I know you from somewhere.
Wait just a minute, don't go anywhere,
I will remember.
I know I know you from somewhere,
I remember now.
As I stand here, looking in the mirror.
You are me.
Where have you been?
I knew that I knew you from somewhere.

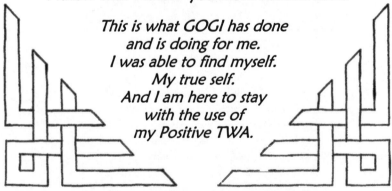

This is what GOGI has done
and is doing for me.
I was able to find myself.
My true self.
And I am here to stay
with the use of
my Positive TWA.

Words from GOGI Girl Maria N.

Knowledge is power and that power is within us all. And united, we can be powerful. Stay positive and live positive. *GOGI for life* ♡

It can be simple, if you only take one day, one thought, one feeling, one action, one day at a time. Love yourself enough to know yourself.

Dedicated to my mother, Lillian V., my grandmother Rosa V. and the Carranza and Vigil Family, always.

Art by Natalie H.

GOGI Coaches celebrate the certification of a GOGI Graduate. Andrea was the first "inmate" to complete her time at the Lynwood county jail and upon her release, dedicate her life to the positive decisions of incarcerated and at risk individuals. Newly certified Coach Andrea successfully completed the GOGI coach training and is well on her way to completing college courses leading to a career as a drug treatment counselor. Not bad work, Andrea! After two decades of incarceration and hardship, you are FINALLY creating the life YOU want!
Go GOGI GIRL Coach Andrea!

CHAPTER 9

REALITY CHECK

It would be nice if change happened immediately and without relapsing into old behaviors. But change can also be a slow process of "two steps forward, one step back." Change may also require constant monitoring until the new habits become automatic.

The unfortunate aspect of our society today is that we go for quick fixes and often give up on our goals during the "one step back" part of the change process. An individual might think, "I promised myself that this time would be different and I failed." Or, maybe, "Obviously, I can never change." If they believe this, they choose not to believe in themselves and are burdened with evidence that they cannot make changes in their behavior.

They might argue by saying, "It's prison. Change is impossible in a place like this," or, "If the situation was more supportive I WOULD change." The point is that everyone has different views and experiences about the process of change. Your perception develops over time. Your experiences create the realities that you experience.

There is no need to feel low or get angry at the world if you "relapse" into old behaviors or beliefs. It may not be optimal, but you can think of falling back into old behavior as a visit down memory lane – and as a place that you do not care to re-experience.

Get yourself out of negative thinking and shame as soon as possible. It's quite probable that you will recover from relinquishing control of your life, and get yourself back into the driver's seat. You can become the boss again.

You can create your life - instead of old habits creating the same negative results.

REALITY CHECK will:

- Help you understand that, "Ten steps forward and two steps back" is sometimes a part of change.

- Help you lighten up on self-criticism and self-blame with the understanding that you can return to your path after a relapse.

- Help you master your process of change and acknowledge that even if it is slow, it may also lead toward lasting freedom.

Words from GOGI Girl Adrienne R.

I'm 25 years old, ingesting drugs that take away my cares of life and excuse me so I can be cold.

I feel untouchable and accustomed to pain, telling myself no one would care if I got slain. Neglected, abused and violated led me to believe that I wasn't loved, but extremely hated.

I was raised in the church, and not a heathen that goes about terrorizing earth. God has a destiny for me that someday I will prevail. I believe that it's not to live my life like I'm in hell.

Why do I constantly choose self-sabotaging behavior? Instead of getting on my knees and talking to my savior? Yeah, indulging in drugs might give me a rush, but when they wear off, it's the eyes and pain of my family who are constantly crushed.

Always a promise that this time, I'll get it right. I pray I will, so I won't be a statistic in a body bag tonight.

THE TRUTH IS. . .

REALITY CHECK
*allows you to remain positive about the
changes that you make in your life.*

REALITY CHECK
*provides you with a "walk down memory lane," gently
reminding you of places that you do not wish to return,
habits that you are leaving behind, and attitudes and
actions that no longer work in your best interest.*

Staying True to what you believe in and
Having an I WANT CHANGE Attitude !!

Words from a GOGI Girl
TRANSITION TO LEADERSHIP

As I sit here at C.R.D.F. thinking about how my life has been, I shrug with chills running through my body and fear falls upon me. As I come to life and my blood begins to flow through my veins, I can feel and hear my heart beat once again.

July 19, 2007 I was arrested. At that time my life seemed as if it had ended. I was ashamed, humiliated, embarrassed and sad. I did not know what was going to happen. I had to pull myself together for whatever decisions my public defender, the District Attorney, and the Judge made, but I was still scared. I didn't want to go to prison, but it was their decision I was worried about.

I was sentenced September 14, 2007 to 270 days at C.R.D.F. For those that don't know, it's 9 months flat. I panicked. I was told by the Judge on April 14, 2008 when I came back to court that I was released.

Despite the panic state, I am now past all of my time. I am now in the month of March 2008 and counting down to the end. This is the longest time I have ever done. Might I say that I have experienced the most by being at C.R.D.F., and hope to never repeat it. But I want to share some of my issues and views with someone that may need a little advice.

In September on the 19th day, I was removed from the 2500 module to the 2200 module pod 4. At that time, it was called the Reach Program. Not knowing what this program was all about, I was basically quiet. Trying to feel and understand what was going on and what it had to offer me.

cont. next page

Transition to Leadership continued

I finally took the time to pray after sitting here in GOGI Campus for about 2 ½ weeks, listening to the other ladies share parts of their life stories. It sure opened my mind, my heart, and my eyes. I felt blind before. My own enthusiasm wanted more to help me see and know and understand what I was going through. I found out that my life story is just as important as theirs, and that everything I do and have done matters.

It helped me to be honest and real to myself, as well as others. I didn't realize how far to the left and what state of mind I was in. I allowed myself to separate from reality and truth. The influences and support I received, along with positive information helped me to stand tall and to thank God for this Reality Check back to a life I once had before my addiction.

GOGI taught me to think before I reach, and also that it takes 21 days to transform a negative habit into something positive and beautiful. Being in control is what it is today. Making the right choices to live a better life. Since I've come to GOGI, in my heart I know I am headed for a new way of life — a better way of living, because I've got the tools.

-- GOGI Campus Student

REALITY Check

Art by Davida M.

HOW DOES REALITY CHECK WORK?

You can focus on the end objective when you understand that change is not always linear or experienced immediately. Set aside any momentary step backward as being an old outdated way of being or behaving.

Think of it like a needle and thread that weaves two pieces of fabric together. The needle is pulled forward, and then is brought back to loop over previously traveled territory before moving forward again. Eventually, the fabric is sewn together. It benefits from a "relapse" of looping over the same sections of fabric it covered previously. It is not an act of failure for the needle to loop over previously sewn fabric.

You can move forward in the larger scheme of things. If you think of those few steps back as visiting a place where you no longer reside or want to be. Let this temporary visit remind you of your significant changes and progress. Continue the delicate dance of restructuring your neurological habits.

ADDED BENEFITS OF REALITY CHECK

It is likely that any relapse of behavior will be shorter, not likely to be repeated, and easier to overcome when you take on the attitude of REALITY CHECK.

HERE'S WHY REALITY CHECK WORKS...

You might label yourself incapable of EVER achieving your objective if you fall into old patterns of behavior and regard yourself as a "loser." Saying "I am a mess up" is a global negative statement. Try saying, "I messed up right now and I won't mess up later."

Reality Check works because you can acknowledge that your behavior is something you can control. Relapse is a temporary visit to a place you no longer live. You can speedily regain control of the steering wheel of your life.

HOW TO DO THE <u>REALITY CHECK</u> TECHNIQUE

You control your actions when you control your thoughts. A major tool in controlling your thoughts is REALITY CHECK. It is a simple way to regain control. Here are the straightforward steps to REALITY CHECK.

STEP 1) REALIZE THAT YOU BACKTRACKED - You must realize, recognize and admit to yourself that you have temporarily returned to an old belief or behavior. Admitting your situation is the "first step" to returning to your desired path.

STEP 2) MEMORY LANE - Understand, and truly believe, the old behavior is a momentary visit down "memory lane." It is <u>not</u> where you want to remain.

STEP 3) FORWARD BENEFITS - Focus on the benefits of change before you get sucked into believing this old behavior holds anything good for you. Ask yourself why you wanted to change in the first place. What do you need to do right now to continue moving forward?

STEP 4) RECOVERY - Grab the wheel of the car, even if you are going 90 miles an hour down a slippery slope. You can slow down with BELLY BREATHING. Get back into control by using any of the tools you have learned.

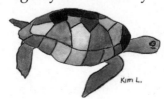

Kim L.

STEP 5) RECOGNIZE - Recognize that you are BOSS OF YOUR BRAIN. Focus on BELLY BREATHING. Use the FIVE SECOND LIGHTSWITCH for new thoughts. Use WHAT IF? to jump start your actions. Focus on POSITIVE TWA.

THINK ABOUT IT

Sometimes your negative or "bad" habits seem impossible to change. People seem to push your buttons even if you are trying to change. Sometimes you are so tired, run down, or discouraged that a slip backwards seems unavoidable. It may seem impossible to give up an unconstructive habit no matter how much better your life would be if you changed.

Take a moment to reflect on some habits that you tried to change. It is likely that you did not quit if you felt that you were being successful in your efforts. It is likely that you started to spiral downward, tossed your hands into the air, and claimed that the habit was in control of you. Or, worse yet, that you never really wanted to give up the habit in the first place. It is likely that you gave up on change when you felt that you had failed or had a relapse. People usually give up prematurely when doing the 10 steps forward and 2 steps back dance of change.

Sometimes, lasting change happens slowly. We all fall down. Just get back on track and keep moving forward. And, go easy on yourself. Just get up quickly and put one foot in front of the next.

WATCH OTHERS

Watch others who attempt to break habits. From observation of the steps they take to break a habit, you might notice that the process is not so easy, but it can be done, it has been done time and time again.

Be careful. Avoid making grandiose proclamations about your goals. Strong statements make it seem like the challenge will be easy to overcome

You may face temptations that are hard to resist. Later, you may make a convincing list of reasons why you are not meeting your goal. Finally, blaming another person or situation starts the cycle over again.

Tread lightly

Women who are successful in breaking habits tend to tread lightly on the issue of their addiction or bad habits. They do not believe that they are invincible. They acknowledge their human frailty when weaknesses surface in the form of old behaviors.

Be gentle with yourself during the process of change. Notice when you feel strong enough to distance yourself from your bad habits. Notice when you feel weak. Take a moment to reflect on what happens when you strongly reinforce new behaviors. With whom do you spend time? What are you thinking and how do you feel? Repeat positive influences as often as you can. Hang with positive people. Being with positive people allows you access to positive words, actions, and conversations.

Walk away from negativity by saying positive things. Read positive materials. Think positive thoughts. Positive invites more positive into your life. Have a goal to break a habit and really work daily to reinforce the goal. Goals help you from being overwhelmed by a momentary, mindless return to a place you no longer want to be. Place yourself in a supportive environment as often as possible.

Remember, people who ultimately change bad habits are those who keep moving forward, even after a setback.

GOGI Girls of GOGI Campus 2008
You can be a GOGI Girl, too. Just know you have sisters out there making the right choices for the right reason. You are not alone. You can change. As difficult as the process may seem, internal freedom is worth the painful process of change...

GOGI Girls of '08

Shannon S
Margaret S
Stepani R
Nacoya H
Tonya H
Elizabeth O
ebony A
Stacy G
Deanna A
Josephina B
Karen R
Keger C
Patricia X B
Sharity A
Margie B

Kimi B
Jennifer B
Dora B B
Charissa C
Andrea W
Felicia "Mimi" J
Wendy L
Stacy P
Elena B
Paula B
Maria C
Shekina R
Kimberly P
Angelina S
Lisa F
Laura A

Erika B   *Sisterhood Love*

A GOGI Girl

What is a GOGI Girl? A GOGI Girl is a woman willing to do whatever it takes to live a life of integrity and honesty. A GOGI Girl is dedicated to a life of service, putting herself in a position to make the world a better place.

Words from GOGI Girl Marguerite S.

It is almost time for me to go home and I have learned so much about how to change my negative thoughts to positive thoughts.

❖ I have learned how to be *The Boss of My Brain.* That means freeing yourself from negative patterns of thinking & allows you to take control of you life.

❖ *Belly Breathing* helps me stay relaxed for better thinking.

❖ Then we have the *5 Second Lightswitch* which will allow me to work with your mind instead of against it. It allows you the ability to control your behavior and help you change undesirable habits.

❖ Another tool is *Positive TWA,* (Thoughts, Words, Actions.) That teaches me how to balance my thoughts and words so that I make more positive statements than negative ones.

❖ Then *What If?* opens my mind to new ideas.

❖ I've learned *Reality Check.* It allows me to remain positive about the changes I'm making in my life, despite slips and setbacks.

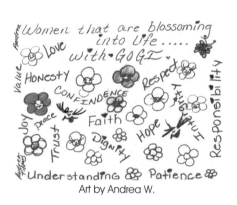

Women that are blossoming into life.....
with GOGI
Love · Value · Honesty · CONFIDENCE · Respect · Joy · peace · Faith · Hope · Trust · Dignity · Responsibility · Understanding · Patience

Art by Andrea W.

CONSIDER THIS...

REALITY CHECK
is a powerful way to get back on track
with your new beliefs and behaviors.
REALITY CHECK
helps remind you of what you really want by allowing you to
temporarily visit a place that you no longer belong.
REALITY CHECK
sees a return to old behavior as a walk down memory lane and
not as a lasting turn of events or failure.

Words from GOGI Girl Angela M.

A Mother's Prayer
Dear God, I hear the chains and feel
fear of the journey that must begin.
I know I'm going to be okay. I know
I'll have a place to stay.
I know I'll get fed every day. That's not my prayer.
For today, you know I've been there. I'll be okay.
My Jesus I pray for my child.
I beg of you to keep her safe.
To guide my daughter's steps.
Don't let her walk the walk I've walked.
Don't let her do the things I've done.
Please Father, guard Brianna's life. She is fragile.
She's been hurt by her mother before.
Dear God, it was my fault.
Please Jesus, work in her a work of mercy.
Through your love, allow my little girl to heal
so she can have the chance in life to
dedicate her voice to you.
Please Father, send her an angel to tuck her in at night.
To kiss her and let her know her mother
prayed for her tonight. Amen.

REALITY CHECK
In Action

LINDA QUITS SMOKING METH

Let's visit our friend, Linda, who has been smoking meth with her brothers since she was 13 years old. She is now 27 years old and has been in trouble with the law since she was 14 for prostitution and stealing to get money to buy speed.

One of the reasons that she smokes is because she does not know how to control her anger. Smoking calms her. All her troubles seem to go away when she is high.

Sometimes she gets so angry that she loses control over her thoughts and actions. Linda knows that she needs to control her anger and quit smoking, but it all seems beyond her control.

Linda just had a fight with her partner. She storms out and heads to her buddy's house. There are several friends there, smoking. Her thoughts drift to, "maybe just one hit."

Let's say Linda forgot to do the BELLY BREATHING. She forgot THE FIVE SECOND LIGHTSWITCH. She ignores her WHAT IF? questions or any other technique that can strengthen her ability to change.

Let's say that she sits down with her friends and gets higher than she has been in months. Eventually she returns home to a disgusted partner and she feels like a loser again.

Art by Davida M.

REALITY CHECK IN ACTION

1) REALIZE THAT YOU BACKTRACKED - First, Linda interprets the night's events as backtracking, and not as a permanent place to where she has returned.

"It's time to think about a sober ME." by Jennifer B.

She backtracked for 8 hours. She realizes that she stayed away from speed for hundreds of hours prior. One hundred hours forward, eight hours back. She reminds herself that she has a commitment to break the habit.

2) MEMORY LANE - A critical element of this technique is for Linda to understand, and truly believe that what she experienced is an old behavior or belief.

It is a mindless return to a place that she no longer wants to be. It is similar to visiting an old school after you have graduated.

3) FORWARD BENEFITS - Before Linda gets sucked into believing that getting high holds anything good for her, she begins to focus on the benefits of change. She remembers why she wanted to change and all the times that she was able to say no. She remembers that she is capable of doing things differently.

To remain on track, she spends less time thinking about what she has done and more time on what to do right now.

4)   RECOVERY - Linda does whatever it takes to return to a positive mental state. She knows that a positive mental state results in positive behavior. When her partner expresses anger, she calmly explains why she is committed to breaking the habit and what the benefits are.

She asks for support to help her return to her desired behavior. She calls her friends and tells them not to take it personally if she does not show up for a while. She needs to quit for good.

5)   RECOGNIZE - Most importantly, Linda can go easy on judging herself as a failure. She knows that it can take a long time to change a habit. If she replaces a negative with a positive, it will only take 21 days to form a new habit. But it requires relentless practice. Regardless of how long it is going to take, she commits to moving forward. Linda does not take her eyes off the long-term benefit of changing her short-term reactions.

WHY IT WORKS

REALITY CHECK is a speedy recovery technique. It empowers you to have a REALITY CHECK when you temporarily return to old and unproductive ways of believing or behaving.

Taking the time to get a REALITY CHECK permits you a realistic perspective on the change process. You can see the distance that you have traveled thus far.

You can focus on all the good that has come out of the changes that you've made. You can review your accomplishments, refocus on them, and know that they are your key to regaining forward momentum once again.

Art by Laura A.

If you go easy on yourself through the process of a reality check, your commitment will strengthen. Look at relapse as a temporary visit to a place that you no longer wish to be, and you will return quicker to the desired behavior.

Words from GOGI Girl Jennifer R.

Jennifer R. by Jennifer B.

GOGI has given me a chance at a new life for which I am truly grateful. I'm here in jail. I'm sober and I am surviving with the tools and support from GOGI. I might get a program, I might go to prison. Either way, GOGI has taught me to be in control of my life. I desperately needed a change and I am lucky to have been given an opportunity at something so useful.

Words from GOGI Girl Sonia A.
It will only take me a minute to pass on what GOGI has made me.

I am:
1. Faster
2. Smarter
3. BETTER
Try it. It works !

Words from GOGI Girl Tonya H.

Here are relapse warning signs for chemical dependency. The following list of relapse warning signs has been developed to help chemically dependent people recognize the typical sequence of problems that leads them from a comfortable and stable recovery back to chemical use.

I know that I truly had an alcohol and/or drug problem. I had a lot of work ahead of me if I was going to truly change myself which meant that I had to work some kind of twelve step program.

I've been in a chronic relapse for the last six years and I am not very happy with myself. I have had opportunities like working as a drug and alcohol specialist for about 6 years and have had sobriety many times, and I ask myself "Why?" This keeps happening and to be as honest as I know how to be.

I can only say everyone's bottom is different; I have been on skid-row eating out of trash cans, been homeless, etc. All these things came with being an addict. I was one of those people who said, "This will never happen to me."

I was told by an old-timer years back that I needed to change one thing. And that was everything. I really don't believe that I listened to what that meant cuz today at 47 years old; I have lost everything one more time and again in jail or prison. If you're anything like me, you know what I mean.

Cont. Next Page

Words from GOGI Girl Tonya H. Continued

Also, I have stepped over the lines and my health isn't the greatest and I can't blame anybody but myself.

Here are just a few things that they suggested I do and where old behavior has to change. Resentments, relationships, internal change, avoidance and defensiveness, denial, crisis-building, immobilization, confusion and over-reaction, depression, behavioral loss of control, alcohol and drug use.

I have experienced those things on a firsthand basis, and I can tell you that they honestly work if you're willing to make the necessary changes to live and not just exist.

Your life will change and now I have had the opportunity to work an even more rewarding program called GOGI. I really believe that this is like the last piece of any 12-step program because it empowers me as a human being to become free from the inside meaning mind, body and soul.

It has taught me that this kind of change can truly last, and I also found a balance within some other things. GOGI has taught me Belly Breathing. I am sure it may sound funny, 'cuz it did to me at first, but it has made such a difference. It calms down your anger if you are having a bad day.

First thing is take a deep breath. With time you'll be doing it and not even know you are. Also, your decision making will be much different as well your choices. You'll be making better choices and getting better results.

Thank you for the opportunity. I will continue to carry GOGI everywhere I go.

OBSERVE OTHERS...

Notice the behavior of others. When people give up on a new habit, take notice when it happened. When you observe others, you are less likely to wallow in self-pity. This does not mean to observe others and blame them for your problems. It means observe and speak with others who have changed a habit, modified a behavior, or reached a goal. You can also observe the struggle of their attempt to do so.

Observing others might mean reading a biography of someone who overcame all odds, or speaking with someone who has risen above addictions.

Also, observe yourself...   ▣   ▣   ▣

When you slide back into old ways of behaving or old beliefs, you can use REALITY CHECK to get yourself back on track. You can also observe your thought patterns, and modify them with a more realistic interpretation of your progress. You will feel powerless if you think that your thoughts are beyond your control, or when you abdicate your right for an amazing life. **The more that you know about yourself the more likely you are to make strong and positive decisions.**

By observing, truly observing, the causes and the effects of the behavior of others, you will undoubtedly feel compelled to walk as far from bad habits as possible.

Get to know yourself. Strengthen yourself from the inside outward. Observe yourself and listen to that still and small voice which only can be heard when you listen and use your GOGI tools.

Words from GOGI Girl Charissa C.

All of my juvenile years, I have been in & out of juvenile halls here in L.A. & in Ventura County. I was in 4 different group homes all over Cali. I did not accept any kind of direction offered. I didn't really believe anyone truly cared.

About 2 months ago, before coming to the GOGI campus, a great friend of mine suggested I read Psalm 51. That particular psalm is a prayer for cleansing from sin. Just what I needed. As I came to verse 13 & read it, visions filled my imagination. Tears streamed down my face because I believed GOD was telling me to get out of the halls & reach out.

As I continued to ponder my dream, I asked questions, "How do I even begin with that?" What do I tell these kids when & if I do get this to become reality? It all just seemed & still does, kind of unrealistic. I just prayed on the entire situation. Well, about a month & a half after all that, the door of opportunity opened. GOGI came into my life. ☺

My 2nd day at GOGI campus, Coach Taylor made one of her uplifting, sincere and radiant talks to us & mentioned about eventually bringing GOGI into juvenile halls & into jails & prisons world-wide. I got goose bumps & butterflies in my tummy when I heard coach say, "Juvi." She also looked right at me as she said it.

My goal is to do exactly that! I want to take GOGI into the exact halls I spent my troubled youth.

I grew up in Ventura County & was very involved in a church. My pastor knows me very well.

Cont. next page

I am in the process of getting my church's address so that I can be spiritually grounded. I am hoping that my church will support me when it comes time to go to the halls, being that I spent a lot of time in Ventura County Juvi. I am very familiar with many of the staff there. So, I figure with the support of my church & being known at VCJH, it will be a smoother ride to get in there. And not only that, but GOGI has my back. My question of what I was going to say is answered. GOGI! Maybe we could even think about making a GOGI youth book. How cool would it be to do that?! Way cool!!!

No matter how long I get sentenced to, whenever I get out, I want to be very much a part of that.

Being a GOGI coach (Coach Charissa) for the youth is my only dream right now. I know I am totally capable of doing that & there is nothing to stop me because I have all the qualifications. I think that maybe if I had someone like Coach Taylor & Coach Liz & GOGI when I was younger, I just might have listened.

-- ♥: Charissa C.

Words from GOGI Girl Laura W.

I am free today because I choose to build bridges over my life's obstacles rather than walling up and shutting down.

Words from GOGI Girl Adrianne K.
GOGI has changed my life.
The past eight years have been dedicated
to going in and out of prison.
This picture was taken during the
four short months between my last prison trip.
GOGI has empowered me,
Changed my life.
Thanks to GOGI,
this is my last trip.
I will never be
away from
my wonderful
family again.
Left to right
(Sister, Crystal,
Brothers
Milton and James.
Then me, Adrianne)
-GOGI is about CHANGE.-

GOGI

Words from GOGI Girl Dora B. D.

When I first got to GOGI, the only thing I was able to do was think of all the negative things that were going on with me.

Then after I read the GOGI book, I was able to start making changes. Some of the tools that helped me are: 5 Second Lightswitch, Boss of Your Brain and Positive TWA.

These 3 tools have taught me how to take a negative thought and turn it into a positive thought.

Which, I must say, has helped me to look at problems that arise in my life a whole new way. A positive way.

Art by Dora B.D.

Art by Laura A.

CHAPTER 10

THE ULTIMATE FREEDOM

TOOLS FOR A GREAT FUTURE

You are not exactly the same individual that you were yesterday. Tomorrow you will not be exactly the same person as you are today.

We may not detect subtle changes that nudge us right or left on life's uncertain crossroads. Changes are often incremental and continual. You create new possibilities as you process each new bit of information, thought or experience. Accumulation of positive information eventually bears the fruit of that tree.

It seems like there needs to be a critical mass of information or experience for a new reality to set in place. You do not go to the gym one time and expect muscles to pop out like a cartoon. Similarly, internal freedom is the result of an accumulation of consistent effort over a period of time.

It is almost impossible to note subtle changes. Good intentions may not have a chance to take root and grow, especially in a fast paced, instant-gratification society. Unfortunately, we seek immediate answers, quick cash, lotto numbers, mega million numbers, magic pills, a silver bullet, or a faster way to move through life. We abdicate our right to create magnificent lives, irrespective of where we live them, when we mistakenly look outside ourselves.

Certain restrictions apply to how fast you can physically move through life during incarceration. You have a precious and valuable opportunity in this imposed slowdown.

You have the opportunity to get out of the human prison and find a rare and powerful freedom. The journey inward is life-long. I do not recall meeting or hearing about any individual who easily found an internal freedom that would effortlessly last a lifetime.

Even in a religious awakening or enlightenment, there is still the need for constant maintenance of the inward journey. There is the need for a relentless practice of shedding perceptions in order to travel inward where the soul resides. Please, take advantage of your incarceration and make this thing called life, work for you. Working toward internal freedom is a natural step that can be included as a part of your daily living.

Here is a reminder for you to keep a watchful eye for when and how possibilities show up in daily experiences.

LET GO

Decide to "free yourself" and you will be able to LET GO of what keeps you from a joyful existence. You will find a way to move beyond old resentments, anger, fear, and unpleasant memories that imprison you. You will find that money, fame, prestige, position, activities and chatter are obstacles to your freedom.

For some women, permission to LET GO and welcome internal freedom comes from a secular (religious) experience. For some, it is facilitated by a spiritual experience that may come from meditation or yoga. For some, the ability to LET GO comes from accumulated data that is presented in books. For some women, it is volunteer work, or focusing on assisting others which permits them to experience LET GO. For some women, LET GO happens when there is no room to go down further into depression and LET GO is the their only hope for living.

LET GO lights the path in the journey to internal freedom.

FORGIVENESS

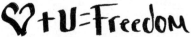

You will notice the act of FORGIVENESS, of self and of others is very freeing. Along the path toward internal freedom there will come a natural, forgiveness which occurs. Somewhere along the journey, you will begin to soften your anger, resentment, bitterness, rage and retaliation. You will come to understand that the longer you hold on to events and actions of the past, it becomes more difficult to move past them into freedom.

When you enter a state of FORGIVENESS, you are able to travel freely and unload the "baggage" of your past. Those who you might find offensive are no longer attached to you or your thoughts. You can let them fend for themselves. Also, in this process of finding internal freedom, there will come a moment when you truly forgive yourself for your own humanness. You will leave behind the heavy load of thinking that you do not have potential for improvement or increased levels of joy and internal freedom. FORGIVENESS of self will permit you to walk beyond the actions and thoughts of the past into a far brighter future. You limit new and different possibilities when you define yourself by prior actions or reactions. To permit FORGIVENESS of self also permits new possibilities of change.

RESPONSIBILITY

The final stage on your journey toward internal freedom is the finest, most empowering experience you can embrace. It is the art of personal RESPONSIBILITY.

You may not feel in control of anything in your life. However, you are completely and totally in control of how you act, re-act, and think about events and situations. In fact, the most out-of-control and unhappy women are those who attempt to control their loved ones. Acting on internal fears, they exert control over their environment by creating rules for those around them. Internal freedom correlates to your level of personal RESPONSIBILITY. With internal freedom, you are not likely to say "You make me mad," or "If you would just..." Actions or reactions do not control the truly free individual. Internally free women assume and welcome total RESPONSIBILITY into their lives.

Everyone is your community. Everyone is on the path. You will only become as free as your muscles of personal RESPONSIBILITY permit you. Take responsibility for your life by letting others take responsibility for their lives.

RESPONSIBILITY allows you to disconnect from the suction cup of emotional control and from others that take away your freedom. These suction cups attach to you, and leave you powerless and imprisoned.

Words from GOGI Girl Sonia A

GOGI is a reminder to take one step at a time so I don't fall. Keep whatever it is that doesn't feel like a GOGI thing to stay away. Be good, look good, feel good. To have a good life, keep on going, with God in my life. When I walk I'll remember to run but I want to get to belly breathe and smile. To help me deal with life, I'll use my tools and with my tools I'll build up my brain and like a light, my life will turn bright. I'll watch and learn how to live a great life!

Words from GOGI Girl Tamesha W.
What Coach means to me.
I met this very special lady.
I thought to myself that I could maybe trust her,
if I could only trust myself.
I let my guard down and I opened my heart.
To my surprise, that was the very first start.
I can't even begin to wonder why.
But every time she came by
there was this ray of sunshine
She doesn't know how special she is to me,
and how GOGI Campus has set me free.
She's more than meets the eye.
More than anyone can see.
She has a smile that can brighten any gloomy day.
She's very educated and knows her way.
She's very spiritual and loves to be of service.
Coach Taylor, you are awesome in so many ways.
You are perfect!

Coach, I can't draw
but thank you for
my life back.

TERI S.

Words from GOGI Girl Dorene M.

Dear Beautiful Lady, Our lives touched for a very very short moment when I was 19 and you were 74. I really want to tell you how very sorry I am; because I tried to steal your purse from you hoping you had money. Enough to buy food. I had been up for 5 days smoking rock cocaine and I had done a little line of speed…that day I tried many ways to obtain some money; none of them the right way.

I didn't think that anyone would give me any money if I just ASKED for it. I tried selling myself for sex for money…I tried trading a fake necklace for rock cocaine…I tried stealing weed from some dealers thinking I could trade the weed so that I could get some cocaine and food to eat…then I tried to steal from a rock cocaine dealer thinking I could smoke some and sell some to get food…none of these ways worked. I was tired and hungry. I didn't even want the cocaine any more. I wish I just asked you for money, I'm sure you would have given me something! I saw you sitting there with your purse and from there we were in a tug of war; pulling the purse back & forth. I didn't want to hurt you in any kind of way.

Beautiful lady, I'm sorry…I can't go back in time and change that moment! I would if it were within my power to do so. I don't know how that moment affected you although I've often thought about it and pray to God that emotionally it wasn't too bad. I am mostly and truly sorry for my actions against you! It is my heart's sincere request to God that you have His peace upon you and have happiness and a constant presence of God, also lots; tons; much joy, and laughter and Love. If you have already passed away, then all my hope and prayers for you is that you had all of the above before you journeyed on from this life here. May you forgive me. With love, DM.

Do not let anyone's behavior, thoughts, actions or reactions alter your course. You must assume total RESPONSIBILITY if you desire internal freedom.

LETTING GO, FORGIVENESS and RESPONSIBILITY are TOOLS that complement the experiences in this book. They help to light your way on your journey toward internal freedom.

Only you can set yourself free

Right now, you hold the keys to your internal freedom. You may not totally believe it. By applying these new tools, you can mold and shape your life experience.

Hold these tools as a core component of who you are and how you live in this world. You will discover how easily change can take place. These tools have the potential to dramatically improve your life, seemingly overnight. In other cases, it will take months or years to find a way into your core. No matter how long it takes, these tools are yours to use as you see fit.

You will pick up new information each time you review this book. Repeat the weekly process as many times as you wish. Practicing the tools will help you to powerfully and positively rework your life. Even if you think that you "got" the information, reread the material and take notes. Like a pro athlete, there is only good which comes from practicing over and over and over again.

Success is a series of Great Defeats. Amber ☺

Words from GOGI Girl Andrea W.

Getting Out by Going In, what a concept to think about. I asked myself, is that even a statement? How do I define GOGI. Getting out of my old behaviors, getting out of my old thinking pattern. How did I do that? By "Going In." Going into my mind and changing the way I thought – replacing my old behaviors with new ones – instead of frowning. I smile now. Instead of thinking I'm a failure, I begin to think that I am an achiever. I can accomplish anything. Replacing my negative thought with positive ones. Going into my inner being – I like to call it "Soul Searching," digging within myself, learning how to let go of my anger, resentments and pain and learning how to forgive myself as well as others. I walked around with a façade for so long until I forgot who I was. Honestly – I really didn't want to remember who I was – because my past was filled with so much guilt, pride and shame. So, I built an unhealthy wall around me called Resentment, Anger and Pain. Because somebody did "Andrea" wrong. But my reality today is more wrong, and it was being done by my own submission – I had some soul searching to do! So, I made a step almost like – step one – I went to the GOGI Campus program. I began working on me with Coach Taylor and other GOGI coaches that I do one-on-one with. I began to absorb what I was listening to and learning to apply it to myself. What I like about GOGI is the support. I feel so much like a part of something special today. Can GOGI help you? I don't know, can it? Only you can help you by wanting to change.

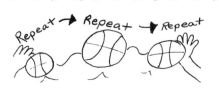

> The simple truth? You are an amazing, powerful force for good. Some part deep inside you is waiting for permission to embrace your internal freedom. Give yourself that permission right now. No one will do it for you. Freedom is yours to claim and to build upon through your journey inward. GETTING OUT of prison BY GOING IN to your internal freedom is your right and privilege.

A Thought from Coach. . .

May God bless you on your journey inward to the only lasting freedom available to mankind. I know this to be true, GETTING OUT BY GOING IN is a universal experience of internal freedom. It is waiting for the spark deep inside you to fuel its fire within.

Continue your journey inward. I will keep you in my prayers that you remain committed to your internal freedom. I ask that you keep me in your prayers as well.

My dedication to this journey inward is undying and relentless but not absent from struggle and heartbreak.

If I feel alone in my journey, the trail might seem uncertain and the path unclear. I often recall my favorite Sufi saying:

"After all this time, the sun has never said to the earth... you owe me."

Let your light shine freely before men. When we love each other in that manner, it lights up the entire world.

After tossing many untruths aside the objective of finding internal freedom is within reach. With any luck, you will discover that the bars of internal imprisonment are actually an illusion.

♥ Love Yourselves! *–GOGI Girl Liliana R.*

Words from GOGI Girl Kim H.

Righting The Wrong Turn.

Another endless day.
I have to find a way to get through this
nightmare.
When all I do is stare at a sea of white walls on
and on, so tall.
This helpless feeling is strong
Where did I go wrong?
I just need to get home and able to freely roam.
To once again be real.
Once more to feel my children's arms around me.
Their mother is what I want to be.
By joining GOGI, I'm righting my wrong.

Art by
Jennifer B.

Words from GOGI Coach Andrea
Dear GOGI Girls,

I hope this brief letter will inspire each of you to want to make change. To those that know me each day has been truly a challenge because I'm learning how to not to act on rejection and dust myself off and try it again. I do by using my GOGI tools. YEAH, it is working for me, WOW!

I attend meetings regularly, I have a sponsor I'm working on the big book. I am here with GOGI on Saturdays and I'm on my way in being a GOGI Coach. I presented my first presentation and of course my favorite one is the 5 Second Lightswitch and being the Boss of my Brain.

The reason why I like the 5 Second Lightswitch is because if your background is anything close to mine then maybe you too can understand. For instance, I been searching for a job since I been home. I turned down one because of the area it was in my old stomping grounds.

I passed that up, and then I had a few other interviews and of course my committee started to work its course and this is where The 5 Second Lightswitch came in to play to allow me to think about all the others that had been shut for only that 5 seconds and swap it on the sixth. And guess what? I start training for a job Wednesday. Yeah!

What I want to say to each of you is that I am doing this I love coming to GOGI for training. Success starts with you, you have to want it. And no matter what keep your heads up. God bless each of you. Love, GOGI Girl ~ Andrea W.

Words from GOGI Girl Yamileth H.

To GOGI and My Kids: *Don't Ever...*

Don't ever try to understand everything.
Some things will just never make sense.
Don't ever be reluctant to show your
feelings. When you're happy, give into it!
When you're not, live with it.
Don't ever be afraid to try to make things better.
You might be surprised at the results.
Don't ever take the weight of the world
on your shoulders.
Don't ever feel guilty about the past.
What's done is done.
Learn from any mistakes you might have made.
Don't ever feel that you are alone.
There is always somebody there for you
to reach out to.
Don't ever forget that you can achieve
so many of the things you can imagine.
Imagine that! It's not as hard as it seems.
Don't ever stop loving.
Don't ever stop believing
Don't ever stop dreaming your dreams.

Let go

forgive

claim responsibility

*GOGI Campus
has showed me how to
have Internal Freedom
and to break through
my chains of bondage.*

Thank you,
Coach Taylor.
By GOGI Girl Wendy R.

I have this wonderful verse in my home:

It is better to light a candle than to curse the darkness.
Anonymous

Light the candle within you. Let it glow and grow with awareness. It leads to new insights, which leads to new behaviors.

Once your candle burns brightly, you can help others to become conscious of their candle. With enough of us helping each other, we can light up the entire world.

Please return to the first page and read the entire book again. And then one more time. You will be amazed at the new information that you learn or pick up from a second, third or fourth reading.

Much love, respect and support for your journey.

Coach Taylor at the GOGI office.

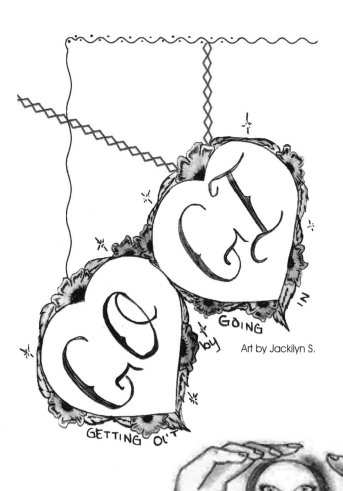

GOING IN

GETTING OUT

by

Art by Jackilyn S.

G.O.G.I.

The Good News is...

Many inmates are ready to integrate all available resources available and are willing to learn how to experience their own internal freedom through thought and behavioral change. It does not take much to make a change when you are ready. In truth, our incarceration system does not provide an environment for positive change for a majority of inmates.

The Federal or State government that has confined you is not obligated to help you find yourself. In truth, many of the individuals working in government are imprisoned themselves. They do not have the tools to find their own internal freedom. How can we expect one group of imprisoned individuals to help another group of imprisoned individuals?

This is your personal journey and, with any luck, when you reach your destination of internal freedom you will extend a hand to the woman next to you. We know what internal freedom "looks" like when we see it in the eyes of someone who has reached their destination. There is no specific roadmap. That is your journey and yours alone.

Those who are released from prison and who positively contribute to society are most likely to make internal changes on their own without the "help" of the current penal system.

No one has more credibility as a force for positive change than someone who has walked your road. You, too, may be a powerful force for good. They can follow in your footsteps if you choose to share your positive transformation with others.

How to Reach GETTING OUT BY GOING IN

Contact GETTING OUT BY GOING IN to request the GOGI books to be shipped free of charge to you, a friend, or family member who is an incarcerated individual.

You may also request information on bringing our programs or speakers to your facility.

Materials in this book were developed with high regard for, *and sincere interest in,* the input and comments of inmates.

Women In Prison: Women Finding Freedom and all books published by GETTING OUT BY GOING IN, are supported by donations. We need your financial support in reaching those who want to change their lives for the better. GOGI is dedicated to the release preparation of incarcerated men, women and youth.

GOGI is a non-profit organization. Donations are tax deductible under section 170 of the Internal Revenue Code: 501c3 #20-3264893.

GETTING OUT BY GOING IN books, workbooks, workshops and classroom settings provide simple tools for making positive choices.

Getting Out

By Going In

E-Mail: info@gettingoutbygoingin.org
Website: www.gettingoutbygoingin.org

GETTING OUT BY GOING IN
PO Box 88969
Los Angeles, CA 90009 USA